Stand Out

Standards-Based English

Rob Jenkins

Staci Lyn Sabbagh

HEINLE & HEINLE

THOMSON LEARNING

Australia • Canada • Mexico • Singapore • Spain • United Kingdom • United States

HEINLE & HEINLE

THOMSON LEARNING

Stand Out 2
Standards-Based English
by Rob Jenkins and Staci Lyn Sabbagh

Acquisitions Editor
Sherrise Roehr

Managing Editor
James W. Brown

Developmental Editor
Ingrid Wisniewska

Associate Developmental Editor
Sarah Barnicle

Editorial Assistant
Elizabeth Allen

Marketing Manager
Eric Bredenberg

Director, Global ESL Training & Development
Evelyn Nelson

Production Editor
Jeff Freeland

Senior Manufacturing Coordinator
Mary Beth Hennebury

Project Manager
Maryellen Killeen

Compositor
TSI Graphics

Text Printer/Binder
Courier

Cover Printer
Phoenix Color Corporation

Designers
Elise Kaiser
Julia Gecha

Cover Designer
Gina Petti

Illustrators
James Edwards represented by Sheryl Beranbaum
Vilma Ortiz-Dillon
Michael DiGiorgio

Cover Art
Diana Ong/SuperStock

For permission to use material from this text or product, contact us by:
Tel   1-800-730-2214
Fax   1-800-730-2215
www.thomsonrights.com

Library of Congress Catalog-in-Publication Data

Jenkins, Rob.
    Stand out 2 : standards-based English / by
    Rob Jenkins and Staci Lyn Sabbagh.—1st
    ed. p. cm.
    Includes index.
    ISBN 0-8384-2217-9
    1. English language—Textbooks for foreign
    speakers. I. Title: Stand out two. II.
    Sabbagh, Staci Lyn. III. Title.

    PE1128 .J435 2002
    428.2'4—dc21
                                    2001039891

Pre-Unit
Page P4: Bill Barley/SuperStock
Page P5a: ©Jack Hollingsworth/CORBIS
Page P5b: Chad Slattery/Tony Stone Images
Page P5c: Owen Franken/CORBIS
Page P5d: Gary Conner/Index Stock Images/PictureQuest

Unit One
Page 1 left: Tony Freeman/PhotoEdit
Page 1 middle: David Katzenstein/CORBIS
Page 1 right: David Young-Wolff/PhotoEdit
Page 2 (all following reading left to right): David Young-Wolff/PhotoEdit; David Katzenstein/CORBIS; Tony Freeman/PhotoEdit; Michael Newman/PhotoEdit; Michael Newman/PictureQuest; Michael Newman/PhotoEdit
Page 3 top left: Corbis Images/PictureQuest
Page 3 top middle: PhotoLink/PictureQuest
Page 3 top right: PhotoDisc
Page 3 bottom left: Douglas Peebles/PictureQuest
Page 3 bottom middle: Digital Vision/PictureQuest
Page 3 bottom right: Photo Sphere Images/PictureQuest
Pages 8 & 9 Ayumi: The Image Bank; Takuya: The Image Bank; Yakari: Bill Bachmann/PhotoEdit; Kenji: David Young-Wolff/PhotoEdit; Akira: Michael Newman/PhotoEdit; Sayuri: Tony Stone; Miyuki: The Image Bank; Ikumi: Michael Newman/PhotoEdit; Yuuki: Mary Kate Denny/PhotoEdit; Tooru: Michael Newman/PhotoEdit
Page 17 Ivan: Catherine Karnow/CORBIS; Anya: David Katzenstein/CORBIS; Alexi and Vladimir: Tony Freeman/PhotoEdit; Irina, Larissa, and Ziven: Myrleen Ferguson Cate/PhotoEdit; Dimitri and Nadia: Michael Newman/PhotoEdit
Page 26 Coins: PhotoDisc

Unit Two
Page 28 top left, bottom left and bottom right: ©Erv Schowengerdt; top middle: Peter Stroumtsos/Alamy.com; top right: CORBIS; bottom middle: PhotoDisc

Unit Three
Page 41 Carrots: Eyewire; Zucchini: CORBIS; Broccoli, Milk, Butter, Cheese, Pasta, Bread, Cereal, Apple, Banana, Orange, Oil, and Soda: ©Erv Schowengerdt; Steak and Candy: PhotoDisc; Chicken: ©Penina/FoodPix; Fish: ©Judd Pilossof/FoodPix.
Page 48 all: ©Erv Schowengerdt
Page 53 top right: Tony Freeman/PhotoEdit; top left and bottom left: SuperStock; middle right: Esbin Anderson/The Image Works; bottom right: ©Bob Daemmerich/The Image Works
Page 57 all: ©Erv Schowengerdt

Unit Four
Page 73 Sofa: ©Elizabeth Whiting & Associates/CORBIS; Lamp and Bookcase: ©Erv Schowengerdt; Chair and Bed: ©Comstock IMAGES; Armchair, Dresser, Dining Room Set, Coffee Table, and Wardrobe: CORBIS

Unit Five
Page 87 left: ©a. g. e. footstock; right: Michael Newman/PhotoEdit

Unit Six
Page 102: ©Bob Daemmrich/The Image Works
Page 104 left and mid-left: Michael Newman/PhotoEdit; mid-right: Dion Ogust/The Image Works; right: ©David Grossman/The Image Works
Page 110 left: SuperStock; right: David White/PhotoEdit
Page 111 top right: ©Aaron Haupt/Stock Boston/PictureQuest; top left: Painet Works, Inc.; bottom left: Novastock/PhotoEdit; bottom right: David Young-Wolff/PhotoEdit

Unit Seven
Page 120: ©Richard Lord/The Image Works
Page 122: Tony Freeman/PhotoEdit
Page 136 top: CORBIS; middle: PhotoDisc; bottom: StockByte
Page 137: Frank Siteman/PhotoEdit

Unit Eight
Pages 155 & 156: Mike McClure/Index Stock Imagery

ACKNOWLEDGMENTS

The authors and publisher would like to thank the following reviewers, consultants, and participants in focus groups:

Elizabeth Aderman
New York City Board of Education, New York, NY

Sharon Baker
Roseville Adult School, Roseville, CA

Lillian Barredo
Stockton School for Adults, Stockton, CA

Linda Boice
Elk Grove Adult Education, Elk Grove, CA

Chan Bostwick
Los Angeles Unified School District, Los Angeles, CA

Rose Cantu
John Jay High School, San Antonio, TX

Toni Chapralis
Fremont School for Adults, Sacramento, CA

Melanie Chitwood
Miami-Dade Community College, Miami, FL

Geri Creamer
Stockton School for Adults, Stockton, CA

Stephanie Daubar
Harry W. Brewster Technical Center, Tampa, FL

Irene Dennis
San Antonio College, San Antonio, TX

Eileen Duffell
P.S. 64, New York, NY

Nancy Dunlap
Northside Independent School District, San Antonio, TX

Gloria Eriksson
Old Marshall Adult Education Center, Sacramento, CA

Marti Estrin
Santa Rosa Junior College, Santa Rosa, CA

Lawrence Fish
Shorefront YM-YWHA English Language Program, Brooklyn, NY

Victoria Florit
Miami-Dade Community College, Miami, FL

Rhoda Gilbert
New York City Board of Education, New York, NY

Kathleen Jimenez
Miami-Dade Community College, Miami, FL

Nancy Jordan
John Jay High School Adult Education, San Antonio, TX

Renee Klosz
Lindsey Hopkins Technical Education Center, Miami, FL

David Lauter
Stockton School for Adults, Stockton, CA

Patricia Long
Old Marshall Adult Education Center, Sacramento, CA

Daniel Loos
Seattle Community College, Seattle, WA

Maria Miranda
Lindsey Hopkins Technical Education Center, Miami, FL

Karen Moore
Stockton School for Adults, Stockton, CA

George Myskiw
Malcolm X College, Chicago, IL

Marta Pitt
Lindsey Hopkins Technical Education Center, Miami, FL

Sylvia Rambach
Stockton School for Adults, Stockton, CA

Charleen Richardson
San Antonio College, San Antonio, TX

Eric Rosenbaum
Bronx Community College, New York, NY

Laura Rowley
Old Marshall Adult Education Center, Sacramento, CA

Amy Schneider
Pacoima Skills Center, Pacoima, CA

Sr. M. B. Theresa Spittle
Stockton School for Adults, Stockton, CA

Andre Sutton
Belmont Adult School, Los Angeles, CA

Jennifer Swoyer
Northside Independent School District, San Antonio, TX

Claire Valier
Palm Beach County School District, West Palm Beach, FL

The authors would like to thank Joel and Roseanne for believing in us, Eric for seeing our vision, Nancy and Sherrise for going to bat for us, and Jim, Ingrid, and Sarah for making the book a reality.

Rob Jenkins

Staci Lyn Sabbagh

I love teaching. I love to see the expressions on my students' faces when the light goes on and their eyes show such sincere joy of learning. I knew the first time I stepped into an ESL classroom that this was where I needed to be and I have never questioned that resolution. I have worked in business, sales, and publishing, and I've found challenge in all, but nothing can compare to the satisfaction of reaching people in such a personal way.

Thanks to my family who have put up with late hours and early mornings, my friends at church who support me, and everyone at CEC who believe in me and are a source of tremendous inspiration.

Ever since I can remember, I've been fascinated with other cultures and languages. I love to travel and every place I go, the first thing I want to do is meet the people, learn their language, and understand their culture. Becoming an ESL teacher was a perfect way to turn what I love to do into my profession. There's nothing more incredible than the exchange of teaching and learning from one another that goes on in an ESL classroom. And there's nothing more rewarding than helping a student succeed.

I would especially like to thank Mom, Dad, CJ, Tete, Eric, my close friends and my CEC family. Your love and support inspired me to do something I never imagined I could. And Rob, thank you for trusting me to be part of such an amazing project.

We are lesson plan enthusiasts! We have learned that good lesson planning makes for effective teaching and, more importantly, good learning. We also believe that learning is stimulated by task-oriented activities in which students find themselves critically laboring over decisions and negotiating meaning from their own personal perspectives.

The need to write **Stand Out** came to us as we were leading a series of teacher workshops, project-based simulations designed to help students apply what they have learned. We began to teach lesson planning within our workshops in order to help teachers see how they could incorporate the activities more effectively. Even though teachers showed great interest in both the projects and planning, they often complained that lesson planning took too much time that they simply didn't have. Another obstacle was that the books available to the instructors were not conducive to planning lessons.

We decided to write our own materials by first writing lesson plans that met specific student-performance objectives. Then we developed the student pages that were needed to make the lesson plans work in the classroom. The student book only came together after the plans! Writing over 300 lesson plans has been a tremendous challenge and has helped us evaluate our own teaching and approach. It is our hope that others will discover the benefits of always following a plan in the classroom and incorporating the strategies we have included in these materials.

ABOUT THE SERIES

The **Stand Out** series is designed to facilitate *active* learning while challenging students to build a nurturing and effective learning community.

The student books are divided into eight distinct units, mirroring competency areas most useful to newcomers. These areas are outlined in CASAS assessment programs and different state model standards for adults. Each unit is then divided into eight lessons and a team project activity. Lessons are driven by performance objectives and are filled with challenging activities that progress from teacher-presented to student-centered tasks.

SUPPLEMENTAL MATERIALS

- The *Stand Out Lesson Planner* is in full color with 77 complete lesson plans, taking the instructor through each stage of a lesson from warm-up and review through application.

- The *Activity Bank CD-ROM* has an abundance of materials, some of which are customizable. Print or download and modify what you need for your particular class.

- The *Stand Out Grammar Challenge* is a workbook that gives additional grammar explanation and practice.

- The *Stand Out* ExamView® Pro *Test Bank CD-ROM* allows you to customize pre- and posttests for each unit as well as a pre- and posttest for the book.

- **The listening scripts** are found in the back of the student book and the Lesson Planner. Cassette tapes and CD-ROMs are available with focused listening activities described in the Lesson Planner.

STAND OUT LESSON PLANNER

The *Stand Out Lesson Planner* is a new and innovative approach. As many seasoned teachers know, good lesson planning can make a substantial difference in the classroom. Students continue coming to class, understanding, applying, and remembering more of what they learn. They are more confident in their learning when good lesson planning techniques are incorporated.

We have developed lesson plans that are designed to be used each day and to reduce preparation time. The planner includes:

- Standard lesson progression (Warm-up and Review, Introduction, Presentation, Practice, Evaluation, and Application)
- A creative and complete way to approach varied class lengths so that each lesson will work within a class period.
- 231 hours of classroom activities
- Time suggestions for each activity
- Pedagogical comments
- Space for teacher notes and future planning
- Identification of SCANS, EFF, and CASAS standards

USER QUESTIONS ABOUT STAND OUT

- **What are SCANS and EFF and how do they integrate into the book?**
  SCANS is the **S**ecretary's **C**ommission on **A**cquiring **N**ecessary **S**kills. SCANS was developed to encourage students to prepare for the workplace. The standards developed through SCANS have been incorporated throughout the **Stand Out** student books and components.

  Stand Out addresses SCANS a little differently than other books. SCANS standards elicit effective teaching strategies by incorporating essential skills such as critical thinking and group work. We have incorporated SCANS standards in every lesson, not isolating these standards in the work unit, as is typically done.

  EFF, or **E**quipped **f**or the **F**uture, is another set of standards established to address students' roles as parents, workers, and citizens, with a vision of student literacy and lifelong learning. **Stand Out** addresses these standards and integrates them into the materials in a similar way to SCANS.

- **What about CASAS?** The federal government has mandated that states show student outcomes as a prerequisite to funding. Some states have incorporated the **C**omprehensive **A**dult **S**tudent **A**ssessment **S**ystem (CASAS) testing to standardize agency reporting. Unfortunately, since many of our students are unfamiliar with standardized testing and therefore struggle with it, adult schools need to develop lesson plans to address specific concerns. **Stand Out** was developed with careful attention to CASAS skill areas in most lessons and performance objectives.

- **Are the tasks too challenging for my students?** Students learn by doing and learn more when challenged. **Stand Out** provides tasks that encourage critical thinking in a variety of ways. The tasks in each lesson move from teacher-directed to student-centered so the learner clearly understands what's expected and is willing to "take a risk." The lessons are expected to be challenging. In this way, students learn that when they work together as a learning community, anything becomes possible. The satisfaction of accomplishing something both as an individual and as a member of a team results in greater confidence and effective learning.

- **Do I need to understand lesson planning to teach from the student book?** If you don't understand lesson planning when you start, you will when you finish! Teaching from **Stand Out** is like a course on lesson planning, especially if you use the Lesson Planner on a daily basis.

  Stand Out does *stand out* because, when we developed this series, we first established performance objectives for each lesson. Then we designed lesson plans, followed by student book pages. The introduction to each lesson varies because different objectives demand different approaches. **Stand Out's** variety of tasks makes learning more interesting for the student.

- **What are team projects?** The final lesson of each unit is a **team project.** This is often a team simulation that incorporates the objectives of the unit and provides an additional opportunity for students to actively apply what they have learned. The project allows students to produce something that represents their progress in learning. These end-of-unit projects were created with a variety of learning styles and individual skills in mind. The team projects can be skipped or simplified, but we encourage instructors to implement them, enriching the overall student experience.

- **What do you mean by a customizable Activity Bank?** Every class, student, teacher, and approach is different. Since no one textbook can meet all these differences, the *Activity Bank CD-ROM* allows you to customize **Stand Out** for your class. You can copy different activities and worksheets from the CD-ROM to your hard drive and then:

  - change items in supplemental vocabulary, grammar, and life skill activities;

  - personalize activities with student names and popular locations in your area;

  - extend every lesson with additional practice where you feel it is most needed.

- **Is this a grammar- or a competency-based series?** This is a competency-based series, with grammar identified more clearly and more boldly than in other similar series. We believe that grammar instruction in context is extremely important. Grammar structures are frequently identified as principal lesson objectives. Students are first provided with context that incorporates the grammar, followed by an explanation and practice. At this level, we expect students to acquire language structure after hearing and reading grammar in useful contexts. For teachers who want to enhance grammar instruction, the *Activity Bank CD-ROM* and/or the *Stand Out Grammar Challenge* workbooks provide ample opportunities.

  The six competencies that drive **Stand Out** are basic communication, consumer economics, community resources, health, occupational knowledge, and lifelong learning (government and law replace lifelong learning in Books 3 and 4).

- **Are there enough activities so I don't have to supplement? Stand Out** stands alone in providing 231 hours of instruction and activities, even without the additional suggestions in the Lesson Planner. The Lesson Planner also shows you how to streamline lessons to provide 115 hours of classwork and still have thorough lessons if you meet less often. When supplementing with the Activity Bank CD-Rom, the ExamView Test Bank CD-Rom, and the Stand Out Grammar Challenge workbooks, you gain unlimited opportunities to extend class hours and provide activities related directly to each lesson objective. Calculate how many hours your class meets in a semester and look to **Stand Out** to address the full class experience.

  Stand Out is a comprehensive approach to adult language learning, meeting needs of students and instructors completely and effectively.

CONTENTS

◆ Grammar points that are explicitly taught. ✤ Grammar points that are presented in context.

EFF	SCANS (Workplace)	MATH	CASAS
• Speak so others can understand; listen actively • Cooperate with others • Take responsibility for learning; reflect and evaluate	• Acquires and evaluates information • Listening • • Speaking • Sociability	• Write numerals 0-30 • Count by 10 to 100 • Write telephone numbers • Fill out a computerized bubble form	**1:** 0.1.1, 0.1.4 **2:** 0.2.1 **3:** 0.1.6 **4:** 0.1.6, 0.2.1 **5:** 0.1.5, 0.1.6, 0.1.2
Most EFF skills are incorporated into this unit, with an emphasis on: • Cooperating with others • Planning (Technology is optional)	Most Scans are incorporated into this unit, with an emphasis on: • Understanding systems • Seeing things in the mind's eye • Self-management • Sociability (Technology is optional)	• Write temperatures using Celsius and Fahrenheit • Interpret and create bar graphs • Tell time with analog clocks • Write times of day in numerals • Discuss time and schedules	**1:** 1.1.3, 2.7.2, 6.7.2 **2:** 1.1.3, 1.1.5, 2.3.3 **3:** 0.1.2, 0.2.1 **4:** 0.1.2 **5:** 0.1.2, 6.7.2 **6:** 2.1.3, 2.3.1 **7:** 7.1.4 **R:** 7.1.4, 7.4.1, 7.5.1 **TP:** 4.8.1, 4.8.5, 4.8.6
Most EFF skills are incorporated into this unit, with an emphasis on: • Using mathematics in problem solving and communication (Technology is optional)	Most Scans are incorporated into this unit, with an emphasis on: • Allocating money • Understanding systems • Arithmetic (Technology is optional)	• Count U.S. money • Say and understand prices • Use addition and multiplication to calculate totals in comparison shopping • Use subtraction to solve real world problems of clothing prices, sales, savings, and discounts	**1:** 1.1.6, 1.2.2, 1.3.9 **2:** 1.3.9 **3:** 1.1.6, 1.3.9, 1.6.4 **4:** 1.3.9 **5:** 1.1.9, 1.1.2 **6:** 1.2.1, 1.2.2, 1.2.3, 1.2.4, 1.3.9, 6.1.1 **7:** 1.1.9, 1.1.2 **R:** 7.1.4, 7.4.1, 7.5.1 **TP:** 4.8.1, 4.8.5, 4.8.6
Most EFF skills are incorporated into this unit, with an emphasis on: • Solving problems and making decisions • Planning • Reflecting and evaluating (Technology is optional)	Most Scans are incorporated into this unit, with an emphasis on: • Decision making • Problem solving • Self-management (Technology is optional)	• Use addition to calculate food price totals on a menu • Use U.S. measurements: pounds, gallons • Use addition to solve cost of food shopping • Present data in bar graphs and Venn diagrams • Budget for food	**1:** 1.3.8 **2:** 1.3.8, 6.1.1 **3:** 1.3.7, 1.3.8 **4:** 1.1.7 **5:** 1.1.3, 3.5.2, 3.5.9, 6.7.2, 6.7.3, 7.4.8 **6:** 1.3.8, 3.5.2, 3.5.9 **7:** 3.5.2, 1.3.8 **R:** 7.1.4, 7.4.1, 7.5.1 **TP:** 4.8.1, 4.8.5, 4.8.6
Most EFF skills are incorporated into this unit, with an emphasis on: • Using mathematics in problem solving and communication • Planning (Technology is optional)	Most Scans are incorporated into this unit, with an emphasis on: • Allocating money • Arithmetic • Creative thinking • Self-management (Technology is optional)	• Compare rent prices for apartments and houses • Fill out a check ledger • Subtract payments from deposits and calculate balance • Write a personal check • Create a monthly budget • Use addition and multiplication to calculate totals	**1:** 1.4.1 **2:** 1.8.1, 1.8.2, 6.1.1, 6.1.2 **3:** 1.4.1 **4:** 1.4.2 **5:** 1.4.2, 1.4.3 **6:** 1.4.1, 6.1.1, 6.1.3 **7:** 1.4.1 **R:** 7.1.4, 7.4.1, 7.5.1 **TP:** 4.8.1, 4.8.5, 4.8.6

CASAS standards: numbers in bold indicate lesson numbers; R indicates review lesson; TP indicates team project.

CONTENTS

◆ Grammar points that are explicitly taught. ❖ Grammar points that are presented in context.

EFF	SCANS (Workplace)	MATH	CASAS
Most EFF skills are incorporated into this unit, with an emphasis on: • Conveying ideas in writing • Speaking so others can understand (Technology is optional)	Most Scans are incorporated into this unit, with an emphasis on: • Acquiring and evaluating information • Writing • Speaking (Technology is optional)	• Interpret a bus schedule • Read phone numbers and addresses and ask about them • Talk about prices of mail and postage • Find out the cost of sending a package overseas	**1:** 2.2.4, 2.2.5 **2:** 0.1.6, 1.1.3, 1.9.4, 2.2.5 **3:** 1.1.3, 1.9.4, 2.2.5 **4:** 1.1.3, 1.9.4, 2.2.1. 2.2.5 **5:** 2.1.1 **7:** 2.4.1, 2.4.2, 2.4.4 **R:** 7.1.4, 7.4.1, 7.5.1 **TP:** 4.8.1, 4.8.5, 4.8.6
Most EFF skills are incorporated into this unit, with an emphasis on: • Solving problems and making decisions • Reflecting and evaluating (Technology is optional)	Most Scans are incorporated into this unit, with an emphasis on: • Understanding systems • Problem solving • Decision making • Self-management (Technology is optional)	• Understand directions related to frequency of taking medications: *2 pills 2 times a day*	**1:** 3.5.9, 7.1.1, 7.1.3 **2:** 3.11, 6.7.2 **3:** 2.1.8, 3.1.2 **4:** 3.1.1, 3.5.9 **5:** 2.1.2, 3.1.1, 3.3.1, 3.3.3 **6:** 3.3.1, 3.3.2, 3.3.3, 3.4.1 **7:** 3.3.1, 3.3.2 **R:** 7.1.4, 7.4.1, 7.5.1 **TP:** 4.8.1, 4.8.5, 4.8.6
Most EFF skills are incorporated into this unit, with an emphasis on: • Solving problems and making decisions • Reflecting and evaluating (Technology is optional)	Most Scans are incorporated into this unit, with an emphasis on: • Organizing and maintaining information • Problem solving • Decision making • Self-management (Technology is optional)	• Present data in the form of a bar graph • Interpret data including dates in an employment application	**1:** 4.4.2, 4.4.4 **2:** 4.1.8, 6.7.2 **3:** 4.1.3, 4.1.9 **4:** 4.1.2, 4.1.5 **5:** 4.1.2, 4.1.8 **6:** 0.2.1, 4.1.5 **7:** 4.5.1, 4.5.4, 4.6.1 **R:** 7.1.4, 7.4.1, 7.5.1 **TP:** 4.8.1, 4.8.5, 4.8.6
Most EFF skills are incorporated into this unit, with an emphasis on: • Planning • Taking responsibility for learning • Reflecting and evaluating (Technology is optional)	Most Scans are incorporated into this unit, with an emphasis on: • Understanding systems • Knowing how to learn • Responsibility • Self-management (Technology is optional)	• Interpret data in a pie chart about education in the United States • Talk about percentages • Understand a timeline setting out goals for the future • Understand data presented as a Venn diagram • Use ordinal numbers	**1:** 7.1.1, 7.5.1 **2:** 1.1.3, 6.7.4, 7.1.1 **3:** 4.4.5, 7.1.1, 7.3.2, 7.5.1 **4:** 7.1.1 **5:** 7.1.1 **6:** 7.1.1 **7:** 2.5.6 **R:** 7.1.4, 7.4.1, 7.5.1 **TP:** 4.8.1, 4.8.5, 4.8.6

CASAS standards: numbers in bold indicate lesson numbers; R indicates review lesson; TP indicates team project.

Guide to Stand Out

Teaching to the Standards has never been easier!

Stand Out is an easy-to-use, standards-based series for adult students that teaches the English skills necessary to be a successful worker, parent, and citizen.

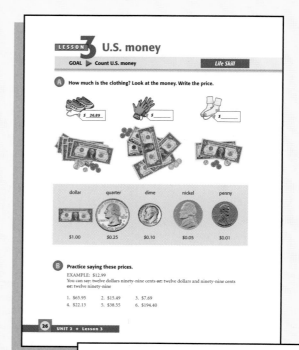

- **Goals:** Provide a road map of learning for the student.

- **Vocabulary:** Introduces key vocabulary visually and aurally.

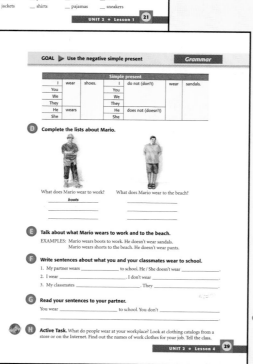

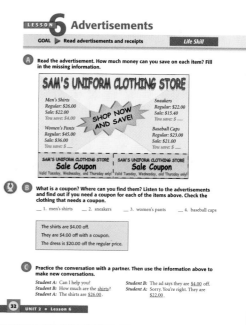

- **Grammar:** Charts clearly explain grammar points, and are followed by personalized exercises.

- **Life Skills:** State- and federally-required life skills and competencies (i.e., EFF, CASAS, SCANS, Model Standards, etc.) are taught, helping students meet necessary benchmarks.

- **Math Skills:** Contextualized math activities are integrated throughout.

Grammar:
Clearly explained and put into immediate use, in this example, with reading and writing.

Review:
Summary of key grammar, vocabulary, and life skills gives students an opportunity to synthesize what they have learned.

Team Projects:
Project-based activities utilize SCANS competencies (e.g., making decisions, working on a team, developing interpersonal skills, etc.) and provide motivation for students.

Pronunciation:
Targets and corrects specific pronunciation problems.

Learner Log:
Final section of each unit provides opportunity for learner self-assessment.

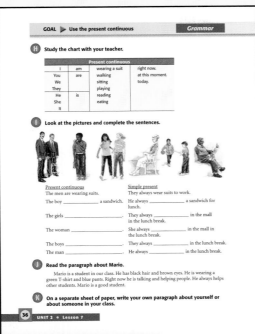

Example pages from the textbook:

GOAL ▶ Use the present continuous — **Grammar**

H Study the chart with your teacher.

Present continuous			
I	am	wearing a suit	right now.
You	are	walking	at this moment.
We		sitting	today.
They		playing	
He	is	reading	
She		eating	
It			

I Look at the pictures and complete the sentences.

Present continuous
The men are wearing suits.
The boy _____ a sandwich.
The girls _____
The woman _____
The boys _____
The man _____

Simple present
They always wear suits to work.
He always _____ a sandwich for lunch.
They always _____ in the mall in the lunch break.
She always _____ in the mall in the lunch break.
They always _____ in the lunch break.
He always _____ in the lunch break.

J Read the paragraph about Mario.

Mario is a student in our class. He has black hair and brown eyes. He is wearing a green T-shirt and blue pants. Right now he is talking and helping people. He always helps other students. Mario is a good student.

K On a separate sheet of paper, write your own paragraph about yourself or about someone in your class.

36 UNIT 2 • Lesson 7

Review

C Write sentences about the people in the picture.

MOUNTAIN VIEW MALL

1. *A man is sitting on a bench. He is wearing an orange sweater.*
2. *A woman* _____
3. *Two boys are* _____
4. *The girl* _____
5. _____
6. _____
7. _____
8. _____

D Complete the paragraph on another sheet of paper.

Many people are at the mall today. Some people are shopping. Two boys are eating pizza. They are wearing baseball caps and jeans.

38 UNIT 2 • Review

TEAM PROJECT

Making your own clothing store

1. Form a team with four or five students. You are going to design your own clothing store.
   In your team, you need:

Position	Job	Student Name
Student 1 Team leader	See that everyone speaks English. Write down ideas.	
Student 2 Artist	Design an advertisement.	
Student 3 Advertising specialist	Write a paragraph with help from the team.	
Student 4 Spokesperson	Prepare a class presentation with help from the team.	

2. Choose a name for your store. What do you sell? Women's clothes? Men's clothes? Children's clothes?
3. Make a list of clothing you sell (8 or more items) on a sheet of paper. Describe the clothing by size, color, pattern, and price. (See pages 30–31.) Are your clothes for work, sports, or school?
4. Cut out pictures or draw pictures of the clothing. Make a newspaper advertisement for your store with pictures of four items or more. (See pages 32 and 37.)
5. Practice asking for prices and selling. (See page 27.)
6. Present the advertisements to the class. For example: Our store's name is _____. We sell _____. This is our advertisement.

UNIT 2 • Team Project 39

PRONUNCIATION

Listen and repeat these prices. Then listen and write the price you hear.

$30 (thirty dollars) – $13 (thirteen dollars) $40 – $14 _____
$50 (fifty dollars) – $15 (fifteen dollars) $70 – $17 _____
$60 (sixty dollars) – $16 (sixteen dollars) $80 – $18 _____

LEARNER LOG

Circle what you learned and write the page number where you learned it.

1. I know words for clothing.
   Yes   Maybe   No   Page _____
2. I can use American money.
   Yes   Maybe   No   Page _____
3. I can read receipts.
   Yes   Maybe   No   Page _____
4. I can describe clothing.
   Yes   Maybe   No   Page _____
5. I can read advertisements.
   Yes   Maybe   No   Page _____
6. I can use the simple present.
   Yes   Maybe   No   Page _____
7. I can use the present continuous.
   Yes   Maybe   No   Page _____
Did you answer No? Review the information with a partner.

Rank what you like to do best from 1 to 6. 1 is your favorite activity. Your teacher will help you.

☐ practice listening
☐ practice speaking
☐ practice reading
☐ practice writing
☐ learn grammar
☐ learn new words (vocabulary)

In the next unit, I want to focus on _____

40 UNIT 2 • Pronunciation and Learner Log

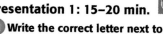

LESSON PLAN

Objectives:
- Identify basic articles of clothing
- Count items of clothing
- Ask and respond to questions

Key vocabulary:

jeans, coats, pants, ties, socks, sweaters, jackets, shirts, pajamas, dresses, hats, raincoats, shoes, skirts, blouses, sneakers

Review of Unit 1: 8–10 min.

Praise students for work on the project and/ or review in Unit 1. Briefly review information learned in Unit 1 using verbs have, be, go and contexts from Unit 1. For example, ask the class: *What time do you go to school? How many sisters do you have? What is the temperature today? Where is (student name) from?* Wait for a few volunteers to answer each question.

ExamView Test Bank Unit 2 Pretest *(optional)*

Warm-up: 10–15 min.

Review the four seasons. Ask the students *What season is it?* Write the seasons across the board. Say what season you like the best. Ask students *Who likes spring best?* Then take a class poll and write the totals on the board under the different seasons.

Introduction: 5–10 min.

Look for a student with a coat. If there is no student with a coat, point to your coat or the one on p. 21. Ask students *In what season do you wear a coat?* Write coat under *winter* on the board. Introduce a few other items of clothing and do the same. **State the objective:** *In this new unit you will learn about words for clothing and about U.S. money.*

Presentation 1: 15–20 min.

A Write the correct letter next to each word.

First look at the picture of the Men's Clothing with the students and have them name the clothing. Note which words the students already know. Label the clothing words with the correct letter from the picture. Practice pronouncing the clothing words.

Practice 1: 20–25 min.

Ask students to form small groups (4–5).

Tell them to choose items from the list in A. Ask students to count the number of people wearing each item of clothing. Have them create or fill out a bar graph with the information as a group. Ask one volunteer from each group to draw the bar graph on the board. Compare answers. Students may have questions about the difference between items (jeans and pants) or about clothing not named on this page. Tell them the names of the items they want to know. Women's clothing will follow on p. 22.

Bar graph Template on Activity Bank CD-ROM. (optional)

STANDARDS CORRELATIONS

CASAS
0.1.2, 0.1.6, 1.3.9, 4.8.1, 6.7

SCANS:
Resources: Allocates Time
Information Acquires and Evaluates Information, Organizes and Maintains Information, Interprets and Communicates Information
Interpersonal Teaches Others
Systems: Understands Systems
Technology Applies Technology to Task *(optional)*
Basic Skills Arithmetic, Listening, Speaking

Thinking Skills Decision Making
Personal Qualities Self-management

EFF:
Communication Speak So Others Can Understand, Listen Actively
Decision Making: Use Mathematics in Problem Solving and Communication, Solve Problems and Make Decisions, Plan
Interpersonal Guide Others, Cooperate with Others
Lifelong Learning Take Responsibility for Learning, Reflect, and Evaluate

---

- **Lesson Plan:** A complete lesson plan for each page in the student book is provided, using nationally-accepted curriculum design.

- **Pacing Guides:** Icon codes offer three different pacing strategies.

- **CD Icon:** Supplemental activities found on the *Activity Bank CD-ROM* are noted with an icon.

- **Warm-up activities** prepare students for lessons.

- **Suggested Internet activities** expose students to technology and real world activities.

A. Counting U.S. money

How many coins and bills do you need for these totals?

Total	$20 bills	$10 bills	$5 bills	$1 bills	quarters	dimes	nickels	pennies
$24.50								
$85.98								
$21.89								
$32.00								
$44.63								
$63.44								

B. Comparing prices

Look at the information and mark the price of each item on the graph. Which store is cheaper?

Sam's Uniform Company
Shirts $14.99
Jeans $25.45
Socks $10.99
Boots $38.00
Jackets $49.50

Mike's Clothing Store
Shirts $19.99
Jeans $23.50
Socks $12.99
Boots $44.00
Jackets $74.50

Copyright © 2002 Heinle & Heinle

Present Continuous and Simple Present

- Use the present continuous with *now, right now, at the moment, today.*
- Use the simple present with *always, often, usually, never, sometimes, every Monday.*

Diem *is working* at the store *right now.* (present continuous)
He *works* at the store *every Thursday.* (simple present)

A Circle the correct verb form.

1. Sam's Uniform Company (is having) / has a sale on shirts and shoes today.
2. Sam always is putting / puts his sale prices on the item tags.
3. He tells / is telling his customers about the sale prices right now.
4. Sometimes Sam's shoes are being / are very expensive for Kenji.
5. Kenji often is using / uses a coupon for $10.00 off the regular price.
6. Today, he spends / is spending only $19.95 with tax.
7. The Nguyen brothers never are reading / read advertisements for clothing.
8. At the moment they look / are looking for new sneakers and boots.
9. Now they ask / are asking Sam about the tax and total price.
10. The Nguyen brothers shop / are shopping every Saturday.

B Complete the sentences with the present continuous or simple present.

1. Duong (wait) ___is waiting___ for his sister outside the department store right now.
2. They usually (go) _____ to the Mountain View Mall at lunchtime.
3. The salesperson (tell) _____ Lien about a sale now.
4. Lien (shop) _____ for a blue skirt today.
5. She never (buy) _____ jeans because she doesn't like them.
6. Every summer Duong (need) _____ a new pair of sandals.
7. Mario and his family always (wear) _____ warm clothes in January.
8. Sometimes Irina and Alexi (spend) _____ too much money for clothes.
9. At the moment, I (walk) _____ around J.D. Allen's Department Store.
10. I often (get) _____ tired because I hate shopping.

Pre-Test Unit 2

A. Read the sales receipts. Then choose the best answer to each question below.

Lydia's Clothes Emporium	Lydia's Clothes Emporium	Lydia's Clothes Emporium	Lydia's Clothes Emporium
1 Socks Size 9-13 $7.45	1 Blouse Size Med $28.99	1 Blue Jeans 34/32 $19.95	1 Shorts Med $16.50
Tax: ....$ .60	Tax: $2.32	Tax: ....$ 1.60	Tax: .... $ 1.32
Total: $8.05	Total: $31.31	Total: $21.55	Total: $17.82

_____ 1. How much is the blouse including tax?

   a. $17.82   c. $31.31
   b. $8.05   d. $28.99

_____ 2. How much are the blue jeans before tax?

   a. $17.82   c. $21.55
   b. $19.95   d. $1.60

_____ 3. You need to pay $8.05 to buy socks. Choose the exact amount below.

   a. Eight dollar bills, one quarter and five pennies.   c. One five-dollar bill, three one-dollar bills, and a dime.
   b. Eight dollar bills, and two quarters.   d. One five-dollar bill, two one-dollar bills, four quarters, and a nickel.

_____ 4. You need to pay $17.82 to buy shorts. Choose the exact amount below.

   a. One ten-dollar bill, one five-dollar bill, two one-dollar bills, two quarters and two pennies.   c. Three five-dollar bills, two one-dollar bills, three quarters, one nickel, and two pennies.
   b. One twenty-dollar bill, two quarters, and a nickel.   d. Seven one-dollar bills, three quarters, and two pennies.

- *Activity Bank CD-ROM:* Hours of motivating and creative reinforcement activities to follow student book lessons are provided. Instructors can download activities and add or adapt them to student needs. The CD-ROM also includes the audio component for listening activities. Cassettes are available for instructors who prefer them.

- *Stand Out Grammar Challenge:* Optional workbook activities provide supplemental exercises for students who desire even more contextual grammar and vocabulary practice.

- *Stand Out ExamView®Pro Test Bank:* Innovative test bank CD-ROM allows for pre- and post-unit quizzes. Teachers can easily print out predetermined tests, or modify them to create their own customized (including computer-based) assessments.

Getting to Know You

GOALS

- Greet your friends
- Describe feelings
- Say letters
- Say numbers
- Follow classroom instructions

LESSON 1 Nice to meet you

GOAL ▶ Greet your friends

Life Skill

A **Practice.**

Mario: Hello, what's your name?
Lien: My name's Lien.
Mario: Nice to meet you, Lien. I'm Mario.

Lien: Hi, Mario. Nice to meet you, too.
Mario: Welcome to our class, Lien.

B **Practice the conversation with five students.**

C **Stand in a line with other students. Stand in alphabetical order by first names.**

GOAL ▶ Describe feelings **Vocabulary**

A **Look at the pictures. Say the words.**

nervous

sad

tired

happy

angry

hungry

B **Practice this conversation.**

You: How are you today?
Your friend: I'm tired.
You: Me too. / Not me. I'm hungry.

C **Ask three students. Write their answers in the chart.**

Student Name	Feelings
Example: Mario	happy

D **Now talk to your friend. Use the names in your chart.**

You: How is Mario today?
Your friend: He's happy. How's Lien?
You: She's nervous.

How do you spell that?

GOAL ▶ **Say letters** | **Life Skill**

A **Listen and practice saying the letters of the alphabet.**

Aa	Bb	Cc	Dd	Ee	Ff	Gg
Hh	Ii	Jj	Kk	Ll	Mm	Nn
Oo	Pp	Qq	Rr	Ss	Tt	Uu
Vv	Ww	Xx	Yy	Zz		

B **Listen and circle the letters you hear.**

1. c   g   d
2. J   G   Z
3. p   b   d
4. F   S   X
5. i   y   j

C **Listen and write the names you hear.**

1. My first name is _____.

2. My last name is _____.

3. I live on _____ Street.

4. I live in _____.

5. I am from _____.

6. My teacher's last name is _____.

D **Work with a partner. Practice spelling your first name, last name, street name, and town or city name.**

LESSON 4 What's your phone number?

GOAL ▶ **Say numbers**   *Life Skill*

A   Listen and practice saying the numbers.

0	1	2	3	4	5	6	7	8	9
10	11	12	13	14	15	16	17	18	19
20	21	22	23	24	25	26	27	28	29
30	40	50	60	70	80	90	100		

B   Listen and write the numbers you hear.

1. _____   3. _____   5. _____   7. _____

2. _____   4. _____   6. _____   8. _____

C   Listen and write the phone numbers you hear.

EXAMPLE: (617) 555-9264

1. _____   3. _____   5. _____

2. _____   4. _____   6. _____

D   Look at the example. Then fill out the form with your telephone number. Write the numbers in the squares and fill in the circles.

EXAMPLE:

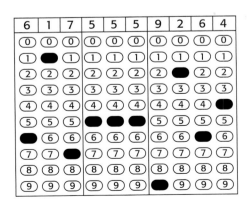

Open your books!

GOAL ▶ **Follow classroom instructions**

A **Match the instructions with the pictures. Write the correct letter next to each sentence.**

a.

c.

b.

d.

_____ 1. Open the book.

_____ 2. Listen to the tape.

_____ 3. Go to the board.

_____ 4. Talk to your partner.

 B **Listen and follow the instructions.**

 C **Listen and repeat. Which of these sentences can you use?**

I'm sorry, I don't understand.

Can you say that again, please?

Can you spell that, please?

Please speak slower.

Please speak louder.

Everyday Life

GOALS

- Talk about places and names
- Talk about weather and seasons
- Use *have* and describe families
- Talk about families
- Describe people
- Talk about time
- Use the simple present

Where are you from?

GOAL ▶ Talk about places and names

Life Skill

 A Look at the map. Draw a line from your country to where you live now.

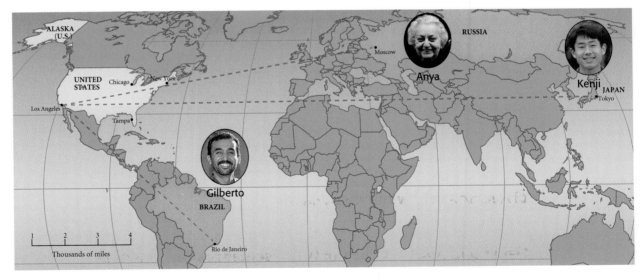

B Write.

EXAMPLE: Kenji is from ___Tokyo, Japan___ . He lives in ___Los Angeles___ .

1. Anya is from ___Moscow Russia___ She lives in ___Los Angeles___ .

2. Gilberto is from ___Rio de Janeiro___ . He lives in ___Los Angeles___

3. I'm from ___Nepal___ . I live in ___Centrevill___ .

C Work in pairs. Ask and answer questions about the students below.

EXAMPLE: *Student A:* Where is Kenji from?
Student B: He is from Tokyo, Japan. Where is Anya from?
Student A: She is from Moscow, Russia.

| Kenji Tokyo, Japan | Anya Moscow, Russia | Gilberto Rio de Janeiro, Brazil | Marie Port-au-Prince, Haiti | Mario Mexico City, Mexico | Lien Ho Chi Minh City, Vietnam |

D Talk to four students in your class. Write the answers in the chart.

EXAMPLE: *Student A:* Excuse me. What's your name?
Student B: My name's Kenji Nakamura.
Student A: Where are you from?
Student B: I'm from Tokyo, Japan.

First Name	Last Name	Town/City	Country
Kenji	Nakamura	Tokyo	Japan
Kim Chi	Nguyen	Saigon	vietnam
Rebeca	Galian	Zacatera	Mexico
Kheng	Lim	phnom	cambida
Kamila	Limbu	kathamandu	nepal

E Make sentences about the people in your class.

EXAMPLE: Kenji Nakamura is from Tokyo, Japan.

GOAL ▶ **Talk about weather and seasons**   *Life Skill*

A **Write the correct word below each picture.**

| sunny | rainy | cloudy | snowy | windy | foggy |

Rainy

Snowy

sunny

Cloudy

wind

foggy

B **Ask your partner questions about the weather.**

EXAMPLE:
Student A: How's the weather today?
Student B: It's sunny.

Student A: Is it cold today?
Student B: Yes, it is. / No, it isn't.

C **Look at the thermometer and complete the chart with the correct numbers.**

Fahrenheit	Celsius
	30°
50° /o	
32° o	
	−15° 3

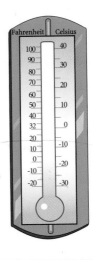

D **What's the temperature today?**

It's ____ degrees Fahrenheit.

E Listen to the world weather report and write the correct temperatures on the map.

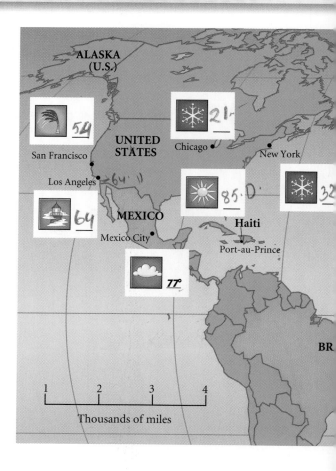

F Work in pairs. Ask questions to fill in your chart. Your partner will look at the map and answer your questions. Then change roles.

EXAMPLE:

Student A: How's the weather in Tokyo?

Student B: It's rainy and 46 degrees.

Student A:

City	Weather	Temperature
Tokyo	rainy	46°
Moscow		
Port-au-Prince		
Ho Chi Minh City		
Los Angeles		

Student B:

City	Weather	Temperature
Mexico City	cloudy	77°
Rio de Janeiro		
New York		
San Francisco		
Chicago		

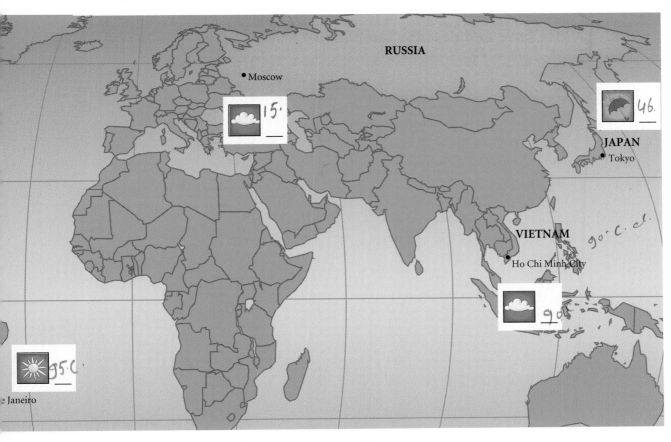

RUSSIA

• Moscow

15·

JAPAN
• Tokyo

46.

VIETNAM

90·C. el.

• Ho Chi Minh City

90

95·C

e Janeiro

G Write the weather for the seasons.

  H **Active Task:** Look in a newspaper or on the Internet and find out about weather in your classmates' countries.

	Chicago	Your School	Your Hometown
SPRING	Windy 60°		
SUMMER	Sunny 83°		
FALL	Cloudy 65°		
WINTER	Snowy 35°		

Kenji Nakamura's family

| GOAL ▶ Use *have* and describe families | *Grammar* |

A **Read Kenji's story.**

My name is Kenji Nakamura. I have a wonderful family. We live in the United States. I have one sister and two brothers. I also have uncles and an aunt here. My father has two brothers and no sisters. My mother has one brother and one sister. My grandparents are in Japan. I'm sad because they are not here with my family.

How many people are in Kenji's family?

B **Complete the sentences.**

EXAMPLE:
Kenji **has** **one** sister.

1. Kenji **has** _____ brothers.

2. Kenji's father _____ _____ brothers and _____ sisters.

3. Kenji's mother _____ _____ sister and _____ brother.

4. Kenji _____ _____ aunt and _____ uncles.

C **Write sentences about your family.**

EXAMPLE:
I **have** **no** sisters.

1. I _have 6_ sister(s) and _NO_ brother(s).

2. My father _has 3_ sister(s) and _2_ brother(s).

3. My mother _has 3_ sister(s) and _2_ brother(s).

4. My parents _have 13_ child (children).

D Study the chart with your teacher.

Have		
I	have	three brothers.
You	have	
He, she, it	has	three children.
We	have	one child.
They	have	

E Complete the sentences.

EXAMPLE: John **has** four brothers and one sister.

1. Thanh ___has___ no sisters.
2. I ___have___ four brothers.
3. Ricardo and Patricia ___have___ seven children.
4. You ___have___ many friends.
5. We ___have___ one child.
6. Maria ___has___ two sisters.

F Talk to four other students and write sentences. Then make a bar graph with names from your class.

EXAMPLE:
Student A: How many brothers and sisters do you have?
Student B: I have three brothers and two sisters.

EXAMPLE:
Juan has three brothers and two sisters.

1. ___I have six sister___
2. ___I have No brother___
3. ___My Housband has five___
4. ___My Housband has 2 sister___

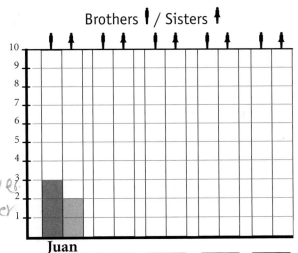

Brothers / Sisters

Juan

G Write a paragraph about your family on a separate piece of paper. Use the sentences from Kenji's story on page 6.

My name is Durga sitaula I have a very nice family we live in united stats I have Two son and one my hasbends and my self My Elder sons school is Liberty middle school. Me is in 8th grade. He wants to be an soccer player. So does little son My little son umamol school is centreridge school

LESSON 4 Family relationships

GOAL ▶ Talk about families

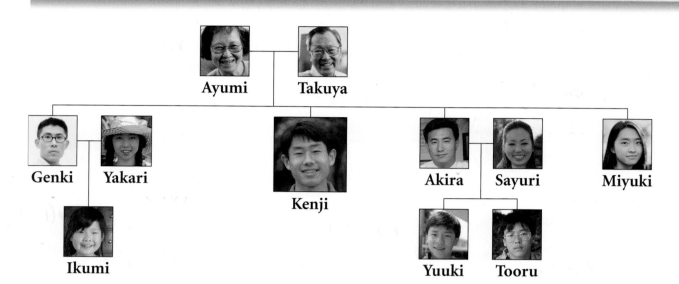

A **Look at Kenji's family tree and answer the questions.**

1. Who are Kenji's brothers? __Akira__, _____.
2. Who is his sister? _____Miyuki
3. Who is Kenji's father? ____Takuya
4. Who is his mother? _____Ayumi
5. Akira is married. Who is his wife? ____Sayuri
6. Who are Akira's children? __Yuuki__, __Tooru__.
7. Who is Yakari's husband? ____Genki
8. Who is single? ____Kenji__, ____Miyuki.

B   **Look at the family tree on page 8 and write the correct words above each picture.**

aunt	niece	daughter	mother
nephew	son	grandfather	father
wife	grandmother	husband	grandson
uncle	parents	children	granddaughter

___*father*___ / ___*son*___   *grandfather* / *granddaughter*   grandmother grand son

Takuya / Kenji   Takuya Ikumi / Ayumi   yuuki

Takuya / Ayumi   Akira / Saymi → yuuki / Tooru

C   **Ask and answer questions about Kenji's family tree.**

Student A: Who are Takuya and Kenji?
Student B: They are father and son.

Student B: Who are Takuya and Ikumi?
Student A: They are grandfather and granddaughter.

D Fill in the chart with your family. Write the names and relationships.

My family chart

My Name: Durga

Spouse: Chetan

My Children:
Asish
Anamol

My Parents:
Father Kul Prasai

Mother Narmaya

Children:
Piyari
Maya
Tanhi
Rupa
Prabati
Durga

My Grandparents:
Grandfather Data Ram prasai

Grandmother Sita prasai

Children:
Lila prasai
Kul Prasai

My Grandparents:
Grandfather D. mainaly

Grandmother Pathak

Children:
Tanka
mankumar

 E Tell a partner or a group about your family.

EXAMPLES:

I have _No_ brother(s) and _six_ sister(s).

My father's name is _Kul Prasad Prasai_.

My mother's name is _Narimaya_.

I have _one_ aunt(s) and _one_ uncles(s).

LESSON 5 Kenji's class

GOAL ▶ **Describe people**

A **Look at the picture and answer the questions.**

How many students are in Kenji's class? Who is tall? Who has blond hair?

He *is* tall and average weight. **Height:** tall, short, average height **Weight:** thin, heavy, average weight	She *has* brown eyes and black hair. **Eyes:** brown, blue, green, gray **Hair:** black, brown, blond, red, gray

B **Make sentences about the students in the picture. Describe their hair, eyes, height, and weight. Use the words in the box.**

EXAMPLE:
  Dalva has green eyes and blond hair.

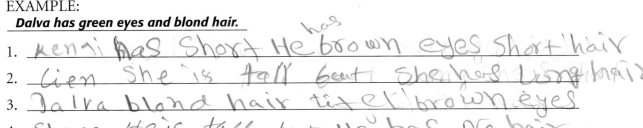

1. Kenji has short He has brown eyes short hair
2. Lien She is tall beut She has Long hair
3. Dalva blond hair titel brown eyes
4. Steve He is tall but He has No hair

C Look at the picture of Kenji's class again. Fill in the graphs about the class.

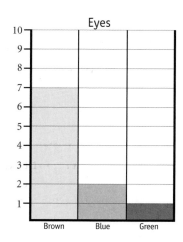

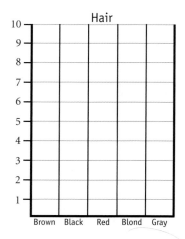

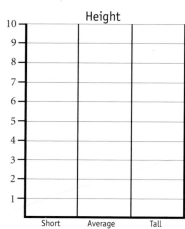

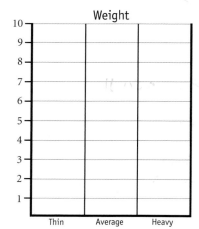

D Write sentences about Kenji's class. Write about *eyes, hair, height,* and *weight.*

EXAMPLE:
Seven students have brown eyes.

_____

_____

_____

E Guess who? Describe a student from Kenji's class. Your partner will guess who it is.

EXAMPLE:
Student A: He's short and heavy. Guess who?
Student B: Mario.

LESSON 6 Time

GOAL ▶ **Talk about time**

A Listen to the conversation and read.

Grandmother: What time is it there?
Kenji: It's 4:00.
Grandmother: In the morning or in the afternoon?
Kenji: In the afternoon. It's 4:00 P.M.
Grandmother: What do you do at 4:00 in the afternoon?
Kenji: I go to school. I go to English class.
Grandmother: OK. Bye, Kenji. Enjoy your class!

B What does Kenji do at 5 A.M.? Look at Kenji's planner and make questions about each time.

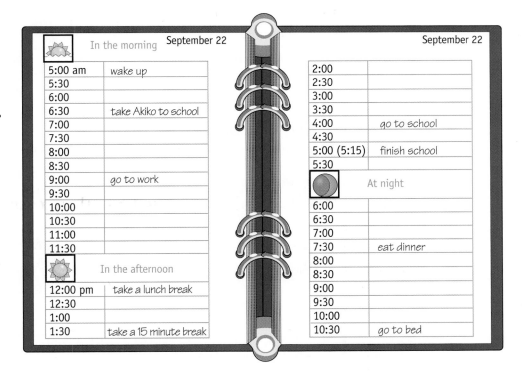

In the morning	September 22
5:00 am	wake up
5:30	
6:00	
6:30	take Akiko to school
7:00	
7:30	
8:00	
8:30	
9:00	go to work
9:30	
10:00	
10:30	
11:00	
11:30	

In the afternoon	
12:00 pm	take a lunch break
12:30	
1:00	
1:30	take a 15 minute break

September 22	
2:00	
2:30	
3:00	
3:30	
4:00	go to school
4:30	
5:00 (5:15)	finish school
5:30	

At night	
6:00	
6:30	
7:00	
7:30	eat dinner
8:00	
8:30	
9:00	
9:30	
10:00	
10:30	go to bed

C You are Kenji. Practice with a partner. Talk about your day.

EXAMPLE:

Student A: What time is it?
Student B: It's ____4:00 P.M.____ .

Student A: What do you do at ____4:00 P.M.____ ?
Student B: ____I go to school____ .

D **Ask your partner about his or her day. Listen and write the information in the planner below. Then change roles.**

EXAMPLE:
Student A:
What do you do
at 8:00 A.M.?
Student B: I eat
breakfast.

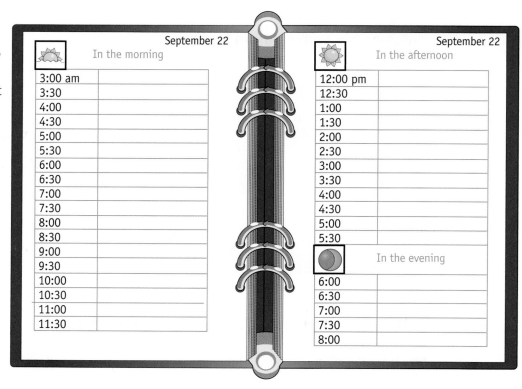

September 22

 In the morning

3:00 am	
3:30	
4:00	
4:30	
5:00	
5:30	
6:00	
6:30	
7:00	
7:30	
8:00	
8:30	
9:00	
9:30	
10:00	
10:30	
11:00	
11:30	

September 22

In the afternoon

12:00 pm	
12:30	
1:00	
1:30	
2:00	
2:30	
3:00	
3:30	
4:00	
4:30	
5:00	
5:30	

In the evening

6:00	
6:30	
7:00	
7:30	
8:00	

E **Write the correct time below each clock.**

5:00 A.M.   _____   _____   _____   _____

 F **Active Task:** Find out about time zones in different countries. Choose one of your classmates' countries. What time is it there now?

LESSON 7 Gilberto's calendar

GOAL ▶ **Use the simple present** *Grammar*

A Read the information on Gilberto's calendar.

Gilberto's Calendar

		Sunday	Monday	Tuesday	Wednesday	Thursday	Friday	Saturday
never	0%			**1** wake up at 5:00 am go to school work	**2** wake up at 5:00 am go to school help with children work	**3** wake up at 5:00 am go to school work	**4** wake up at 5:00 am go to school work	**5** wake up at 5:00 am work overtime
rarely								
sometimes	50%	**6** wake up at 6:00 am play soccer	**7** wake up at 5:00 am go to school help with children work	**8** wake up at 5:00 am go to school work	**9** wake up at 5:00 am go to school help with children work	**10** wake up at 5:00 am go to school work	**11** wake up at 5:00 am go to school work	**12** wake up at 5:00 am go to school take bus to the beach
often		**13** wake up at 6:00 am play soccer	**14** wake up at 5:00 am go to school help with children work	**15** wake up at 5:00 am go to school work	**16** wake up at 5:00 am go to school help with children work	**17** wake up at 5:00 am go to school work	**18** wake up at 5:00 am go to school work	**19** wake up at 5:00 am work overtime
always	100%							

B Answer the questions.

1. What does Gilberto do Monday to Friday?
   a) He goes to the beach.
   b) He works and goes to school.
   c) He plays soccer.

2. What does he do every Monday and Wednesday?
   a) He helps with the children.
   b) He works overtime.
   c) He wakes up at 7:00 A.M.

C Are these sentences true or false? Circle the correct answer.

1. Gilberto sometimes goes to work on Saturday.   True   False

2. He never plays soccer on Sunday.   True   False

3. He always gets up at 5 A.M.   True   False

4. He often helps with the children.   True   False

Study the charts with your teacher.

Regular Verbs		
I	work	at 8:00 A.M.
You	work	
He, she, it	work<u>s</u>	
We	work	
They	work	

I work at 8:00 A.M.
She works at 8:00 A.M.

Have		
I	have	three children.
You	have	
He, she, it	ha<u>s</u>	free time.
We	have	
They	have	

I have three children.
She has free time.

Go		
I	go	to school.
You	go	to the beach.
He, she, it	go<u>es</u>	to work.
We	go	
They	go	

I go to school.
She goes to the beach.

Be		
I	am	Gilberto.
You	are	a cook.
He, she, it	is	happy.
We	are	
They	are	

I am a cook.
He is Gilberto.
We are happy.

 Change the sentences from *I* to *He.*

EXAMPLE: I often go to school.
    He often goes to school.

1. I sometimes help with the children.

   _____

2. I always wake up at 5:00 A.M.

   _____

3. I rarely go to the beach.

   _____

4. I never work on Sunday.

   _____

F **Fill in the missing words.**

EXAMPLE: Gilberto and I **_are_** (be)
good friends.

1. Gilberto _____ (be) always busy.

2. We both _____ (work) on
   weekdays.

3. After school, he _____ (go) to
   work.

4. I _____ (go) to school also.

5. He _____ (help) his wife with
   the children.

6. They _____ (take) the
   children to school.

Review

A Look at Anya's family tree and write the relationships.

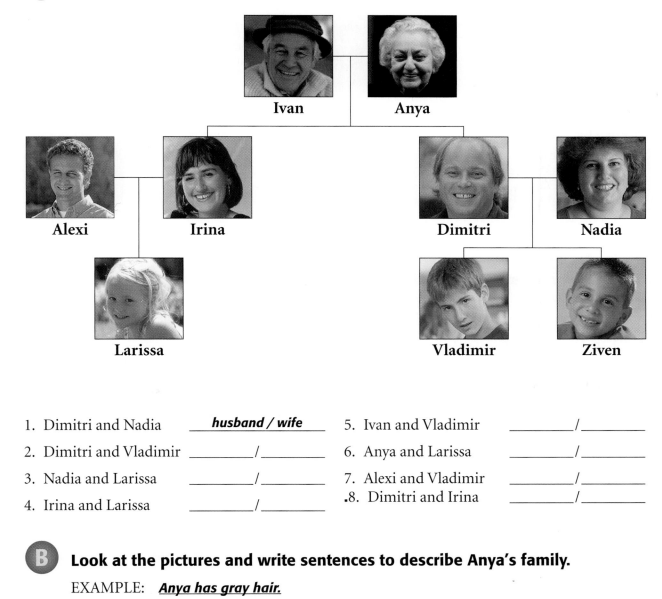

Ivan   Anya

Alexi   Irina   Dimitri   Nadia

Larissa   Vladimir   Ziven

1. Dimitri and Nadia   __husband / wife__   5. Ivan and Vladimir   _____/_____

2. Dimitri and Vladimir   _____/_____   6. Anya and Larissa   _____/_____

3. Nadia and Larissa   _____/_____   7. Alexi and Vladimir   _____/_____

4. Irina and Larissa   _____/_____   .8. Dimitri and Irina   _____/_____

B Look at the pictures and write sentences to describe Anya's family.

EXAMPLE: ___Anya has gray hair.___

1. _____   3. _____

2. _____   4. _____

Larissa's Planner

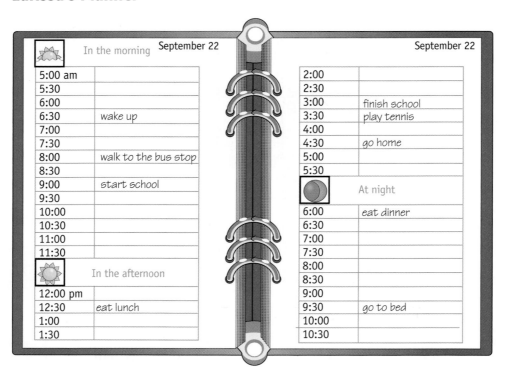

		September 22
☀	In the morning	
5:00 am		
5:30		
6:00		
6:30	wake up	
7:00		
7:30		
8:00	walk to the bus stop	
8:30		
9:00	start school	
9:30		
10:00		
10:30		
11:00		
11:30		
☀	In the afternoon	
12:00 pm		
12:30	eat lunch	
1:00		
1:30		

		September 22
2:00		
2:30		
3:00	finish school	
3:30	play tennis	
4:00		
4:30	go home	
5:00		
5:30		
●	At night	
6:00	eat dinner	
6:30		
7:00		
7:30		
8:00		
8:30		
9:00		
9:30	go to bed	
10:00		
10:30		

C **Describe Larissa's day. Write four sentences.**

EXAMPLE:
Larissa wakes up at 6:30 A.M.

1. _____

2. _____

3. _____

4. _____

D **Complete the paragraph with the correct form of *be* or *have*.**

My name __*is*__ Larissa. I _____ a wonderful family. We _____ happy in the United States. My father's name _____ Alexi. He _____ tall. He _____ blond hair. My mother's name _____ Irina. She _____ short. She _____ brown hair. My parents _____ brown eyes. I _____ blond hair and I _____ short.

T E A M
P R O J E C T

Describing a student

1. Form a team with four or five students. You are going to describe a student from your group or a student from page 11.

   In your team, you need:

Position	Job	Student Name
Student 1 Team leader	See that everyone speaks English. See that everyone participates.	
Student 2	Write a paragraph with help from the team.	
Student 3	Make a family tree with help from the team.	
Student 4	Make a calendar and a one-day planner with help from the team.	

2. Choose a student from your group or a student from page 11 (not Kenji or Anya).

3. Write a paragraph about the student's family. (See page 6 for help.)
   Where is the student from?
   Where does he or she live now?
   How many brothers and sisters does he or she have?

4. Make a family tree for the student. (See pages 8 and 17 for help.)

5. Make a one-day planner for the student. (See pages 13–14 for help.)

6. Make a calendar for one month. (See page 15 for help.)

7. Report to the class.

Listen to the questions and repeat.

1. What is your name?
2. Who is she?
3. Where are they from?

4. What is your job?
5. Who are they?
6. Where are you from?

LEARNER LOG

Circle what you learned and write the page number where you learned it.

1. I can ask *Where are you from?*
   Yes   Maybe   No   Page _____

2. I can read a map.
   Yes   Maybe   No   Page _____

3. I can talk about the weather.
   Yes   Maybe   No   Page _____

4. I can talk about families.
   Yes   Maybe   No   Page _____

5. I can describe people.
   Yes   Maybe   No   Page _____

6. I can tell the time.
   Yes   Maybe   No   Page _____

7. I can talk about my schedule.
   Yes   Maybe   No   Page _____

Did you answer *No?* Review the information with a partner.

Rank what you like to do best from 1 to 6. 1 is your favorite activity. Your teacher will help you.

- [ ] practice listening
- [ ] practice speaking
- [ ] practice reading
- [ ] practice writing
- [ ] learn grammar
- [ ] learn new words (vocabulary)

In the next unit, I want to focus on

_____ (e.g., listening,

speaking, grammar).

Time to Go Shopping

GOALS

- Identify clothing
- Ask about prices
- Count U.S. money

- Use the negative simple present
- Describe clothing
- Read advertisements and receipts
- Use the present continuous

LESSON 1

Shopping for clothes

GOAL ▶ Identify clothing

Vocabulary

A **Write the correct letter next to each word.**

| __ jeans | __ coats | __ pants | __ ties | __ socks |
| __ sweaters | __ jackets | __ shirts | __ pajamas | __ sneakers |

B **Write the correct letter next to each word.**

__ dresses   __ hats   __ raincoats

__ shoes   __ skirts   __ pants

__ blouses   __ shirts   __ sneakers

C Look at the examples and write the correct words below each picture.

EXAMPLES:

<u>   one sock   </u>

<u>a pair of socks</u>

<u> three socks </u>

1. _____

3. _____

5. _____

2. _____

4. _____

6. _____

D Work in pairs. Take turns asking questions about the clothing on pages 21 and 22.

EXAMPLE:
Student A: How many coats are there?   *Student B:* Three
Student B: How many pairs of shoes are there?   *Student A:* One

E Write 3 items of clothing you are wearing today.

1. _____

2. _____

3. _____

How much is it?

GOAL ▶ **Ask about prices**

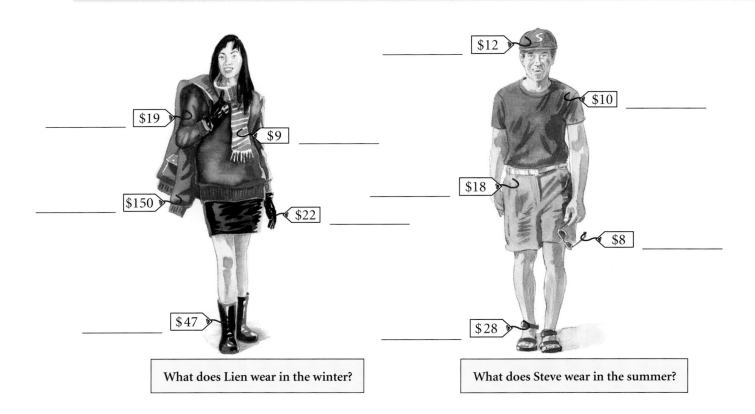

$12

$10

$19

$9

$150

$18

$22

$47

$8

$28

What does Lien wear in the winter?

What does Steve wear in the summer?

A **Write the words from the box next to the correct clothing above.**

T-shirt	coat	gloves	scarf	sunglasses
boots	sweater	sandals	shorts	baseball cap

B **Work in pairs. Ask and answer questions about the pictures.**

EXAMPLE:

Student A: How much is Lien's scarf?   *Student B:* It's $9.

Student B: How much are Steve's sunglasses?   *Student A:* They're $8.

C **What is the total cost of each person's clothing?**

How much are Lien's winter clothes? _____

How much are Steve's summer clothes? _____

Student A: Ask your partner about the prices of clothing for winter (coat, gloves, scarf, boots, sweater). Listen to your partner and write the words and prices on the line from cheap to expensive.
Student B: Look at page 24 and answer student A's questions.

EXAMPLE: *Student A:* How much is the coat?
          Student B: (Look at page 24.) It's $150.
          Student A writes: coat ($150).

coat ($150)

cheap   expensive

 Student B: Ask your partner about the prices of clothing for summer (sunglasses, shorts, sandals, T-shirt, baseball cap). Listen to your partner and write the words and prices on the line from cheap to expensive.
Student A: Look at page 24 and answer student B's questions.

EXAMPLE: *Student B:* How much are the sunglasses?
          Student A: (Look at page 24.) They're $8.
          Student B writes: sunglasses ($8).

sunglasses ($8)

cheap   expensive

 What clothing do you need right now? You have $300. Make a list.

Items	Price
	$
	$
	$
	$
	$
	$
Total:	$

GOAL ▶ Count U.S. money

A How much is the clothing? Look at the money. Write the price.

$ __26.89__

$ _____

$ _____

dollar	quarter	dime	nickel	penny
$1.00	$0.25	$0.10	$0.05	$0.01

B Practice saying these prices.

EXAMPLE: $12.99
You can say: twelve dollars ninety-nine cents **or:** twelve dollars and ninety-nine cents
or: twelve ninety-nine

1. $65.95   2. $15.49   3. $7.69
4. $22.13   5. $38.55   6. $194.40

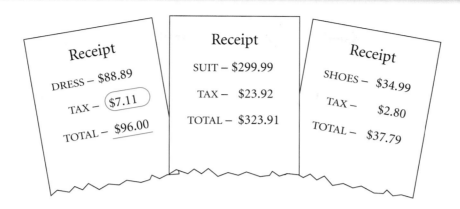

Receipt

DRESS – $88.89

TAX – $7.11

TOTAL – $96.00

Receipt

SUIT – $299.99

TAX – $23.92

TOTAL – $323.91

Receipt

SHOES – $34.99

TAX – $2.80

TOTAL – $37.79

C **Answer the questions for each receipt with a partner.**

1. How much is the <u>dress</u>? _____

2. How much is the tax? _____

3. How much is the total? _____

How much is this shirt?

How much are these shoes?

D **Listen to the dialogue and make similar conversations with a partner.**

Customer: Excuse me. How much is this shirt?
Salesperson: It's $24.99.
Customer: How much is that with tax?
Salesperson: That's $26.25 with tax.
Customer: Fine! / No, thanks, that's too expensive.

What do they wear in winter?

GOAL ▶ Use the negative simple present

A **Look at the picture and answer the questions.**

> Where does the Hernandez family live?
> What season is it?
> Do you like this season?

B **Read the paragraph.**

This is the Hernandez family. Mario is the husband. Teresa is his wife. They have a beautiful 11-month-old baby daughter. Her name is Graciela. They don't have any sons. They moved from Mexico to Chicago in summer. Now it's winter and it's hot in Mexico, but it's cold in Chicago. Mario and his family wear warm clothes in Chicago in winter. They don't wear shorts and they don't wear sandals in winter. The Hernandez family likes Chicago, but they don't like winter.

C **What does the family wear in winter? Ask a partner.**

EXAMPLE: *Student A:* What does Mario wear in winter?
Student B: He wears a coat. He doesn't wear shorts.

Mario	Teresa	Mario and Teresa
Mario wears a coat in winter.	_____	_____
He doesn't wear shorts.	_____	_____

Simple present						
I	wear	shoes.	I	do not (don't)	wear	sandals.
You			You			
We			We			
They			They			
He	wears		He	does not (doesn't)		
She			She			

D **Complete the lists about Mario.**

What does Mario wear to work?

_____ ***boots*** _____

_____

_____

What does Mario wear to the beach?

_____

_____

_____

E **Talk about what Mario wears to work and to the beach.**

EXAMPLES: Mario wears boots to work. He doesn't wear sandals.
Mario wears shorts to the beach. He doesn't wear pants.

F **Write sentences about what you and your classmates wear to school.**

1. My partner wears _____ to school. He / She doesn't wear _____.

2. I wear _____. I don't wear _____.

3. My classmates _____. They _____.

G **Read your sentences to your partner.**

You wear _____ to school. You don't _____

_____.

H **Active Task:** What do people wear at your workplace? Look at clothing catalogs from a store or on the Internet. Find out the names of work clothes for your job. Tell the class.

What are they wearing?

GOAL ▶ **Describe clothing**   *Vocabulary*

A Look at the sizes, colors, and patterns below.

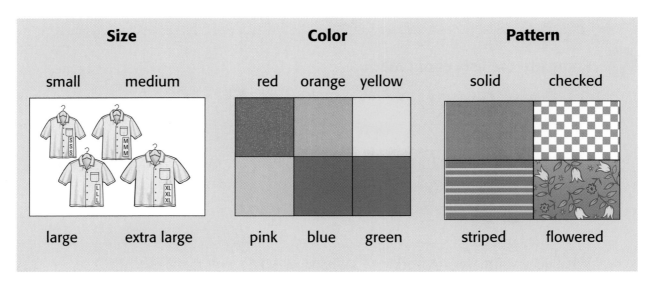

Size	Color	Pattern
small medium	red orange yellow	solid checked
large extra large	pink blue green	striped flowered

The Nguyen Brothers

So   Duong   Tan   Diem

B What are the brothers wearing today? Talk in a group.

C Listen and write the name of one of the brothers.

1. ___*Diem*___   3. _____   5. _____

2. _____   4. _____   6. _____

D **Write two sentences about each brother.**

1. *So is wearing an extra large, blue, striped shirt today.* _____

   _____

2. *Duong* _____

   _____

3. *Tan* _____

   _____

4. *Diem* _____

   _____

E **Write a paragraph about the Nguyen family. Review describing people's appearance from pages 11–12.**

The Nguyen brothers are from Vietnam. So is tall and heavy. He is wearing an extra large,

blue, striped shirt. Duong is _____

_____

_____

_____

_____

_____

_____

F **Describe yourself and what you are wearing.**

_____

_____

_____

_____

_____

_____

_____

_____

Advertisements

GOAL ▶ Read advertisements and receipts	*Life Skill*

A Read the advertisement. How much money can you save on each item? Fill in the missing information.

SAM'S UNIFORM CLOTHING STORE

Men's Shirts
Regular: $26.00
Sale: $22.00
You save: $4.00

SHOP NOW AND SAVE!

Sneakers
Regular: $22.00
Sale: $15.40
You save: $ —

Women's Pants
Regular: $45.00
Sale: $36.00
You save: $ —

Baseball Caps
Regular: $23.00
Sale: $21.00
You save: $ —

SAM'S UNIFORM CLOTHING STORE **Sale Coupon** Valid Tuesday, Wednesday, and Thursday only!	SAM'S UNIFORM CLOTHING STORE **Sale Coupon** Valid Tuesday, Wednesday, and Thursday only!

B What is a coupon? Where can you find them? Listen to the advertisements and find out if you need a coupon for each of the items above. Check the clothing that needs a coupon.

___ 1. men's shirts   ___ 2. sneakers   ___ 3. women's pants   ___ 4. baseball caps

> The shirts are $4.00 off.
>
> They are $4.00 off with a coupon.
>
> The shirts are $4.00 off the regular price.

C Practice the conversation with a partner. Then use the information above to make new conversations.

Student A: Can I help you?
Student B: How much are the <u>shirts</u>?
Student A: The shirts are <u>$26.00</u>.

Student B: The ad says they are <u>$4.00</u> off.
Student A: Sorry. You're right. They are <u>$22.00</u>.

D This is Mario and Teresa's receipt for work clothes. Read the information and answer the questions. Then fill in the receipt using the information on page 32.

E Answer the questions.

1. How many shirts are on the receipt? _____

2. What does *Unit Price* mean?
   a) how many
   b) how much for one
   c) total price

3. What does *Item* mean?
   a) the price
   b) how many
   c) kind of clothing

4. What does *Grand Total* mean?
   a) price for all items
   b) coupon price
   c) number of clothes

Sam's Uniform Company
20 Row St, Chicago IL 80000

Quantity	Item	Unit Price	Total
3	Men's shirts	$_____	$_____
2	Women's pants	$_____	$_____
1	Men's boots	$_48_	$_____
2	Women's belts	$_18_	$_____
		Grand Total	$_____

F Fill in the receipt.

Addy's Clothing Company
25 Row St, Chicago IL 80000

Quantity	Item	Unit Price	Total
2	Men's shirts	$32.00	$_____
4	Women's pants	$34.00	$_____
1	Men's boots	$37.00	$_____
1	Women's belts	$16.00	$_____
		Grand Total	$_____

G Look at both receipts in your group. What store has good prices? What clothing store has good prices in your city?

 H **Active Task:** Go to two clothing stores near your home or on the Internet. Choose one item of clothing and compare the prices. Tell the class.

LESSON 7
What to wear for work and school

GOAL ▶ **Use the present continuous**

Grammar

A Look at the pictures and describe what the people are wearing.

B Listen and read.

Irina, her husband Alexi and their daughter Larissa are from Russia. They live in New York City. They want to buy clothes for work and for school. They are looking at a flyer to see what people are wearing. They are talking about the clothing.

Mountain View Mall

| Men's and Women's Career Wear | School Clothing |

| Teens' Dress and Casual Clothing | Men's and Women's Work Clothing |

Visit our Pet Department!

C Close your books and listen. Then read the conversation with your teacher.

Irina: Look. All the children are wearing T-shirts.

Larissa: No, Mom. That girl is wearing a dress.

Irina: Larissa, many girls in the U.S. wear pants for school.

Alexi: These children are wearing backpacks like children in Russia.

Larissa: Mom and Dad, I want to buy a pair of pants, some T-shirts, a backpack, and a dress. OK?

Alexi: That sounds good. Now, what are we wearing to work, Irina?

Irina: Well, you need a suit for your work. I need jeans and boots for my job.

Larissa: Look at this dog. It's wearing a sweater!

Present continuous			
subject	+ (be)	+ verb + *ing*	
It	is	wearing	a sweater.

D **Write sentences about the people in the pictures on page 34.**

1. Alexi is wearing _____

2. Irina and Larissa are wearing _____

3. The children _____

4. A woman _____

5. A man _____

6. A man and a woman _____

E **Talk to two students. Say what they are wearing. Write sentences.**

You are wearing _____

_____

_____

_____

F **Look for students who are wearing the same clothes in your class. Write sentences.**

1. _____ and _____ are wearing the same thing.

   They are wearing _____.

2. _____ and _____ are wearing the same thing.

   They are wearing _____.

G **What are you wearing?**

I am wearing _____.

I _____.

H **Study the chart with your teacher.**

Present continuous			
I	am	wearing a suit	right now.
You	are	walking	at this moment.
We		sitting	today.
They		playing	
He	is	reading	
She		eating	
It			

I **Look at the pictures and complete the sentences.**

Present continuous

The men are wearing suits.

The boy _____ a sandwich.

The girls _____.

The woman _____.

The boys _____.

The man _____.

Simple present

They always wear suits to work.

He always _____ a sandwich for lunch.

They always _____ in the mall on their lunch break.

She always _____ in the mall on her lunch break.

They always _____ on their lunch break.

He always _____ on his lunch break.

J **Read the paragraph about Mario.**

Mario is a student in our class. He has black hair and brown eyes. He is wearing a green T-shirt and blue pants. Right now he is talking and helping people. He always helps other students. Mario is a good student.

K **On a separate sheet of paper, write your own paragraph about yourself or about someone in your class.**

A   Look at the advertisements.

1.

SALE PRICE
$22

Regular price $25

ALL SIZES

No coupon required

2.

SALE PRICE
$15
with coupon

Regular price $25

ALL SIZES AND COLORS

3.

SALE PRICE
$45

Regular price $52

SMALL SIZES ONLY

Coupon required

4.

SALE PRICE
$14

Regular price $28

M AND L ONLY

Color: Blue solid

5.

SALE PRICE
$24

Savings: $5

**ALL MEN'S AND
WOMEN'S SIZES**

No coupon necessary

6.

SALE PRICE
$34
with coupon

Regular price $44

**ALL SIZES OF
WOMEN'S SHOES**

B   Fill in the missing information.

1. Item: __blue jeans__
   Coupon: Yes (No)
   Color: __blue__
   Pattern: __solid__
   Size: __all__
   Sale Price $__22__
   Regular Price $__25__
   Savings: $ __3__

2. Item: _____
   Coupon: Yes   No
   Color: _____
   Pattern: _____
   Size: _____
   Sale Price $_____
   Regular Price $_____
   Savings: $ _____

3. Item: _____
   Coupon: Yes   No
   Color: _____
   Pattern: _____
   Size: _____
   Sale Price $_____
   Regular Price $_____
   Savings: $ _____

4. Item: _____
   Coupon: Yes   No
   Color: _____
   Pattern: _____
   Size: _____
   Sale Price $_____
   Regular Price $_____
   Savings: $ _____

5. Item: _____
   Coupon: Yes   No
   Color: _____
   Pattern: _____
   Size: _____
   Sale Price $_____
   Regular Price $_____
   Savings: $ _____

6. Item: _____
   Coupon: Yes   No
   Color: _____
   Pattern: _____
   Size: _____
   Sale Price $_____
   Regular Price $_____
   Savings: $ _____

C Write sentences about the people in the picture.

1. *A man is sitting on a bench. He is wearing an orange sweater.*
2. *A woman*
3. *Two boys are*
4. *The girl*
5. _____
6. _____
7. _____
8. _____

D Complete the paragraph on another sheet of paper.

Many people are at the mall today. Some people are shopping. Two boys are eating pizza. They are wearing baseball caps and jeans.

Making your own clothing store

1. Form a team with four or five students.
   You are going to design your own
   clothing store.

   In your team, you need:

Position	Job	Student Name
Student 1 Team leader	See that everyone speaks English. See that everyone participates.	
Student 2 Artist	Design an advertisement.	
Student 3 Sales specialist	Write a conversation and practice it with the team.	
Student 4 Spokesperson	Prepare a class presentation with help from the team.	

2. Choose a name for your store. What do you sell? Women's clothes? Men's clothes? Children's clothes?

3. Make a list of clothing you sell (8 or more items) on a sheet of paper. Describe the clothing by size, color, pattern, and price. (See pages 30–31.) Are your clothes for work, sports, or school?

4. Cut out pictures or draw pictures of the clothing. Make a newspaper advertisement for your store with pictures of four items or more. (See pages 32 and 37.)

5. Practice asking for prices and selling. (See page 27.)

6. Present the advertisements to the class. For example: *Our store's name is _____. We sell _____. This is our advertisement.*

PRONUNCIATION

Listen and repeat these prices. Then listen and write the price you hear.

$30 (thirty dollars) – $13 (thirteen dollars) $40 – $14 _____

$50 (fifty dollars) – $15 (fifteen dollars) $70 – $17 _____

$60 (sixty dollars) – $16 (sixteen dollars) $80 – $18 _____

LEARNER LOG

Circle what you learned and write the page number where you learned it.

1. I know words for clothing.
   Yes   Maybe   No   Page _____

2. I can use American money.
   Yes   Maybe   No   Page _____

3. I can read receipts.
   Yes   Maybe   No   Page _____

4. I can describe clothing.
   Yes   Maybe   No   Page _____

5. I can read advertisements.
   Yes   Maybe   No   Page _____

6. I can use the simple present.
   Yes   Maybe   No   Page _____

7. I can use the present continuous.
   Yes   Maybe   No   Page _____

Did you answer *No?* Review the information with a partner.

Rank what you like to do best from 1 to 6. 1 is your favorite activity. Your teacher will help you.

☐ practice listening

☐ practice speaking

☐ practice reading

☐ practice writing

☐ learn grammar

☐ learn new words (vocabulary)

In the next unit, I want to focus on

_____.

UNIT

Food and Nutrition

GOALS

- Identify food groups
- Read a menu
- Follow directions in a supermarket
- Use count and non-count nouns
- Talk about nutrition
- Plan meals
- Use the negative simple present

LESSON 1 What do you eat?

GOAL ▶ Identify food groups   *Life Skill*

A Label the food groups with the words below.

Breads, grains	Fruit	~~Vegetables~~	Dairy	Meat	Fats, oils, sweets

Vegetables _____

_____

_____

_____

_____

_____

B Name each of the foods above.

C Which foods are more important in your diet? Rank the food groups from 1–6 (1 = most important) and give examples of each group. Compare your answers with other students.

____ Meat _____

____ Vegetables _____

____ Fruit _____

____ Breads and grains _____

____ Dairy _____

____ Fats, oils, and sweets _____

D Look at what Gilberto is eating for lunch. What are the food groups? Complete the list.

lettuce _____*Vegetables*_____

beef _____

bun _____

tomato _____

E What did you eat today? Name five things and check the food groups.

Food Items	Meat	Vegetables	Fruit	Breads, Grains	Dairy	Fats, Oils, Sweets

LESSON 2 — Augustin's restaurant

GOAL ▶ Read a menu

Vocabulary

Augustin's Restaurant
Lunch Menu

Sandwiches
Big burger $2.98 Big burger cheeseburger $3.49
Super burger combo $5.99
Turkey sandwich $2.25

Main Courses
(All main courses come with a vegetable)
Sirloin steak and potatoes $8.50
Fried chicken and french fries $5.99

Soups and Salads
Caesar salad $2.49   Dinner salad $1.85   Potato soup $1.49

Side Orders
French fries $1.85   Potato chips $0.85
Vegetable of the day $2.00   Rice $1.25
Beans $1.25

Beverages
Cola, Root beer $1.19   Milk $1.29   Coffee $2.00   Tea $1.75

Dessert
Chocolate cake $2.75   Vanilla ice cream $1.75
Cheesecake $2.00   Fruit of the day $2.00

A Look at the menu and write your order for lunch. What kind of soup or salad /side order/ beverage/dessert do you want?

_____

_____

_____

_____

_____

_____

B Listen to these people in a restaurant. What do they want to eat? Write down their orders. Then find out the cost of each order.

Table Number 1	
1 Super Burger Combo	$ *5.99*
1 dinner salad	$ *1.85*
_____	$_____
_____	$_____
_____	$_____
Total	$_____

Table Number 3	
_____	$_____
_____	$_____
_____	$_____
_____	$_____
_____	$_____
Total	$_____

Table Number 6	
_____	$_____
_____	$_____
_____	$_____
_____	$_____
_____	$_____
Total	$_____

Where is Gilberto?
What is his job?
What is he cooking?

 C **Close your books and listen to Gilberto's story.**
Then open your books and read about Gilberto.

I am a cook in my father's restaurant. His name is Augustin. My name is Gilberto. My mother, sister, and brother work here, too. We have American food at our restaurant. I want to have some food from other countries, too. Maybe someday we can have an international restaurant.

D **Circle the correct answer.**

1. Gilberto works in a restaurant.	True	False
2. Gilberto only cooks American food.	True	False
3. His two sisters work in the restaurant too.	True	False
4. He wants the restaurant to have food from many different countries.	True	False

E **Make a list of food from your country and share it with the class.**

Rice   Curry   pulse   Ricepudding
Chicken Tandory   medet
Momo   Sale   Roti   Sekuwa
Chowmein pulau   Palak paner
Kuplilo

F In a group, make an international menu. Write the name of your restaurant at the top. Fill in the blanks under the parts of the menu.

_____   _____

Main Courses

_____ . . . . . . $_____

_____ . . . . . . $_____

Soups and Salads

_____ . . . . . . $_____

_____ . . . . . . $_____

Sandwiches

_____ . . . . . . $_____

_____ . . . . . . $_____

Side Orders

_____ . . . . . . $_____

_____ . . . . . . $_____

Beverages

_____ . . . . . . $_____

_____ . . . . . . $_____

Desserts

_____ . . . . . . $_____

_____ . . . . . . $_____

G Practice these conversations in your group. Use the information from your new menu to make conversations.

Conversation 1:
Server: Can I take your order?
Customer: Yes, what's the <u>soup</u> today?
Server: <u>Won ton soup</u>.
Customer: That sounds great. I'll take that.

Conversation 2:
Server: Can I take your order?
Customer: Yes, I'll have _____ and _____.
Server: Anything else?
Customer: That's all thanks.

 H **Active Task:** Go to a restaurant near your home or on the Internet. Find a menu and bring it to class.

GOAL ▶ Follow directions in a supermarket   **Vocabulary**

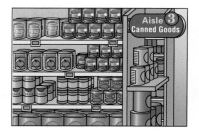

A In what section and what aisle can you find these items? Look at the picture and complete the chart.

Item	Section	Aisle
flour	Baking goods	
milk		
tomatoes		
meat		

B Read about Augustin's problem.

Augustin goes to the supermarket every Friday to buy food for his family. Today they need milk, tomatoes, and bread. His wife also wants him to get flour and two cake mixes. Augustin needs help to find the flour and the cake mixes.

Singular	Plural
Where **is** the flour?	Where **are** the cake mixes?
It **is** in aisle 4.	They **are** in aisle 4.

C Practice the conversation with a partner.

Use these words: milk, tomatoes, canned corn, chicken, pears, ice cream, butter, soup, sugar, oranges.

EXAMPLE:
Augustin: Excuse me. Where is the <u>flour</u>?
Assistant: <u>It's</u> in aisle 4.

Augustin: Where <u>are</u> the <u>cake mixes</u>?
Assistant: <u>They are</u> also in aisle 4.

D **Look at the diagram below. Fill in the circles with names of supermarket sections and food you can buy in them.**

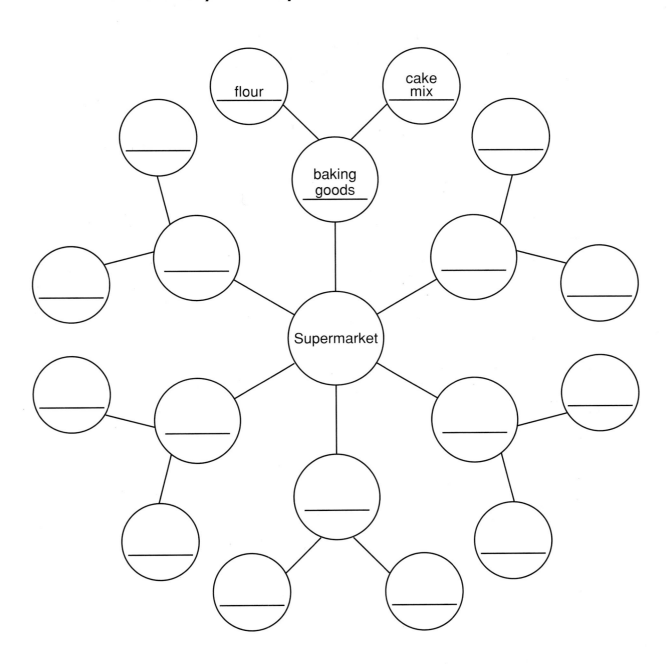

GOAL ▶ **Use count and non-count nouns**   **Grammar**

 A Complete Augustin's shopping list with the words from the pictures.

carton(s)

pound(s)

jar(s)

bottle(s)

box(es)

loaf(loaves)

bag(s)

can(s)

gallon(s)

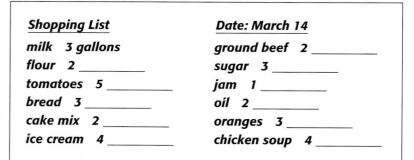

Shopping List		Date: March 14	
milk	3 gallons	ground beef	2 _____
flour	2 _____	sugar	3 _____
tomatoes	5 _____	jam	1 _____
bread	3 _____	oil	2 _____
cake mix	2 _____	oranges	3 _____
ice cream	4 _____	chicken soup	4 _____

B Practice this conversation with a partner, using the words from the shopping list.

EXAMPLE:

Augustin: What do we need at the store?
Silvia: We need <u>some milk</u>.
Augustin: How many <u>gallons</u> do we need?
Silvia: We need <u>three gallons</u>.

C Study the boxes with your teacher. Look back at the food on page 48. Which kinds of food are count nouns and which are non-count nouns?

Count nouns	Non-count nouns
Use *many* with nouns you can count.	Use *much* with nouns you cannot count.

D Look at the examples and complete the sentences, using *much* or *many.*

EXAMPLES:
How ***many*** tomatoes do we need?　　　　How ***much*** flour do we need?
How ***many*** pounds of tomatoes do we need?　　How ***many*** bags of flour do we need?

1. How _____ bananas do we need?

2. How _____ bottles of oil do we need?

3. How _____ oil do we need?

4. How _____ flour do we need?

5. How _____ apples do we need?

6. How _____ pounds of apples do we need?

E You are making hamburgers for 20 people. You also need chips and drinks. In groups, make a shopping list. How much do you need?

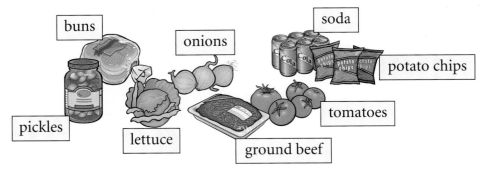

buns　onions　soda　potato chips　pickles　lettuce　ground beef　tomatoes

 F **Active Task:** Go to your local market or use the Internet to find the total cost of your food items.

Shopping list	
_____	_____
_____	_____
_____	_____
_____	_____

The nutrition pyramid

GOAL ▶ Talk about nutrition	*Vocabulary*

A Look at exercise C on page 42 again. Tell the class about types of food that are important for you.

B Look at the nutrition pyramid. The pyramid shows that we need to eat more of some foods and not so much of other foods.

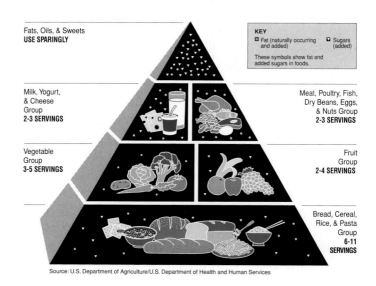

Food Guide Pyramid
A Guide to Daily Food Choices

Fats, Oils, & Sweets
USE SPARINGLY

KEY
▢ Fat (naturally occurring and added)   ▢ Sugars (added)
These symbols show fat and added sugars in foods.

Milk, Yogurt, & Cheese Group
2-3 SERVINGS

Meat, Poultry, Fish, Dry Beans, Eggs, & Nuts Group
2-3 SERVINGS

Vegetable Group
3-5 SERVINGS

Fruit Group
2-4 SERVINGS

Bread, Cereal, Rice, & Pasta Group
6-11 SERVINGS

Source: U.S. Department of Agriculture/U.S. Department of Health and Human Services

C Which food groups are healthy for us?
Rank the food groups from 1–6. 1 = very healthy.

____ Meat
____ Dairy
____ Vegetables
____ Breads, Grains
____ Fruit
____ Fats, Oils, and Sweets

D Use the information from the pyramid to complete the bar graph about nutrition. How many servings of each food group do we need every day?

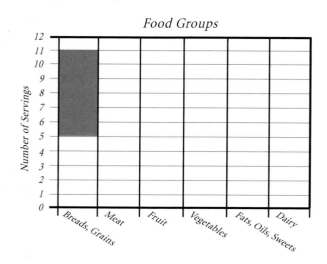

Food Groups

Number of Servings

Breads, Grains   Meat   Fruit   Vegetables   Fats, Oils, Sweets   Dairy

E   **Listen with your books closed. Then read the paragraph and circle the correct answer.**

Nutrition means the food we eat and how much we eat of each food group. Good nutrition is important. When we eat good food, our bodies are stronger and we stay healthy. The nutrition pyramid is a guide that helps us choose the best food for a balanced diet. It is healthy to eat food from each of the main food groups.

1. A balanced diet is the same as a healthy diet.	Yes	No
2. The nutrition pyramid tells us what to eat every day.	Yes	No
3. It is healthy to eat food from each food group.	Yes	No
4. It is healthy to eat a lot of food from each food group.	Yes	No

F   **How much of each food group do you eat every week? Complete these sentences for yourself.**

I eat a little of _____. I eat about _____ servings every week.

I eat a lot of _____. I eat about _____ servings every week.

G   **Ask three students about what they eat and fill in the chart.**

EXAMPLE:
You: What do you eat a lot of?
Susan: I eat a lot of bread.

You: What do you eat a little of?
Susan: I eat a little fat and oil.

Name	A lot of	A little of
1. Susan	bread	fat and oil
2.		
3.		
4.		

Augustin's Restaurant
Breakfast Menu

Eggs & More
two eggs $2.99
steak and eggs $7.50
ham and eggs $4.50
cereal $1.50
6 pancakes $2.50

Sides
2 slices of toast . . . . $ .99
hash brown potatoes $1.25
fresh fruit $2.50
4 slices of bacon $1.50

Beverages
milk $1.19
orange juice $1.75
apple juice $1.70
coffee $1.00

H **Read the menu and check the correct food group for each type of food.**

Food Items	Meat	Vegetables	Fruit	Breads, Grains	Dairy	Fats, Oils, Sweets
bacon	X					
cereal						
eggs						
fresh fruit						
ham						
hash browns						
milk						
orange juice						
steak						
toast						

I **Make a list of the kind of foods you eat for breakfast. Tell your partner. Your partner will identify the food group for each kind of food.**

My breakfast

1. _____

2. _____

3. _____

4. _____

Food group

_____

_____

_____

_____

6 Augustin's family

GOAL ▶ **Plan meals**

Gilberto

Breakfast	— donut and coffee
Lunch	— hamburger, fries and cola
Dinner	— cheese and pepperoni pizza and beer

Augustin's family works very hard at the restaurant.
They don't eat together because they don't have time. What do they eat?

Silvia

Breakfast	— cereal and milk
Lunch	— green salad and fruit juice
Dinner	— spaghetti with meatballs and ice cream

Rosa

Breakfast	— toast and coffee
Lunch	— soup, bread, fruit and yogurt
Dinner	— turkey, potatoes, green salad and water

Fernando

Breakfast	— fruit, cereal, milk and toast
Lunch	— pepperoni pizza and milk
Dinner	— fried chicken and baked potato

Augustin

Breakfast	— coffee
Lunch	— sausage, beans, rice and water
Dinner	— cheese, bread, green salad and fruit

 A **Talk with a partner. Ask questions about the pictures.**

EXAMPLE:
Student A: What does Silvia eat for lunch?
Student B: She eats a green salad and drinks fruit juice.

Student A: What does Augustin eat for breakfast?
Student B: He drinks coffee.

B **Who do you think has the best nutrition? In a group rank the family from 1–5. 1 = the best nutrition.**

____ Augustin
____ Silvia
____ Gilberto
____ Rosa
____ Fernando

C Write the foods Rosa and Augustin eat for breakfast, lunch, and dinner in the circles. Look at the examples.

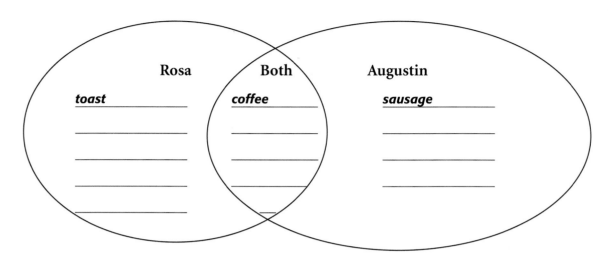

Rosa   Both   Augustin

toast _____   *coffee* _____   *sausage* _____

_____   _____   _____

_____   _____   _____

_____   _____

_____

D What do you and your family eat for breakfast, lunch, and dinner? Complete the chart.

Breakfast	Lunch	Dinner

E Talk to a partner.

EXAMPLE:

Student A: What do you eat for breakfast? Lunch? Dinner?

Student B: I eat _____. I drink _____.

Making a shopping list

GOAL ▶ **Use the negative simple present**   *Grammar*

Where are Augustin and Silvia?
What are they doing?
What are they saying?

A   Read.

Augustin and Silvia make a shopping list for the restaurant every Thursday morning. On Thursday they are not busy. This week they already have a lot of food. They don't need to buy very much.

B   What do Augustin and Silvia need?
Listen and put a check next to the items below.

> ***Shopping List***
>
> ☑ *Ground beef*   ☐ *turkey*   ☐ *ham*
> ☐ *bacon*   ☐ *tuna fish*   ☐ *chicken*
> ☐ *lettuce*   ☐ *tomatoes*   ☐ *carrots*
> ☐ *fresh fruit*   ☐ *sugar*   ☐ *flour*

C   Write sentences about the shopping list.

EXAMPLE: ***They need ground beef. They don't need tomatoes.***

_____

_____

_____

_____

_____

_____

Study the chart with your teacher.

Regular Verbs: Negative simple present			
I	do not	need	lamb.
You	(don't)	want	tuna fish.
We		have	turkey.
They			
He	does not		
She	(doesn't)		
It			

Be: Negative simple present		
I	am (I'm) not	hungry.
You	are not	happy.
We	(aren't)	angry.
They		busy.
He	is not	tired.
She	(isn't)	
It		

 Write the sentences in the negative.

1. They have turkey for dinner.
   They don't have turkey for dinner.

2. He needs bread.

   _____

3. You need bacon.

   _____

4. I want breakfast right now.

   _____

5. We have fish every Friday.

   _____

6. I am hungry.

   _____

7. You are very busy.

   _____

8. They are good workers.

   _____

9. Silvia is very organized.

   _____

10. We are tired of this food.

    _____

 You and your group are going to prepare a healthy and nutritious dinner. Make a list of five kinds of food you need and five kinds of food you don't need. Report to the class.

Review

A Draw a line from the picture to the correct word. Write the food name under the picture.

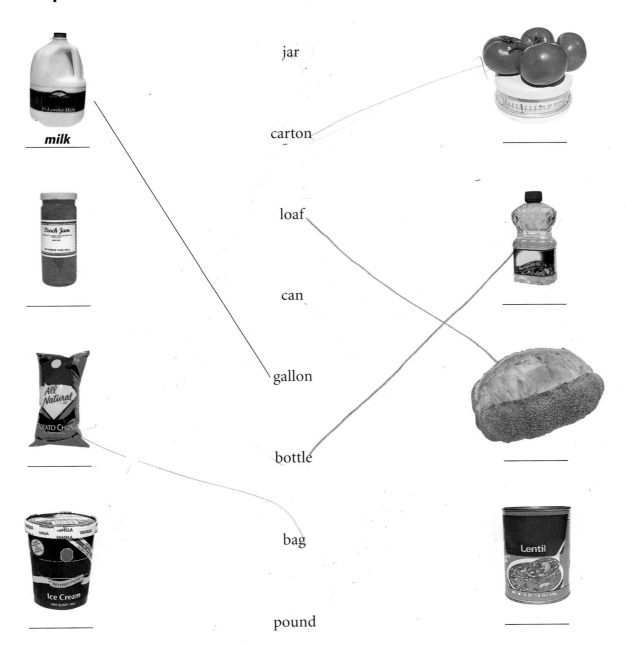

jar

carton

_____

loaf

_____

can

gallon

bottle

_____

bag

_____

pound

__milk__

_____

_____

B Look at the menu. Fill in the name for each part of the menu. Look at page 45 for help.

MENU

_____   _____

Vegetable and choice of potato included.

Grilled chicken	$7.49	Roast lamb	$15.89
Sirloin steak	$15.95		

_____

Baked potato	$2.50	Cola, mineral water	$1.19
Vegetable of the day	$2.00	Coffee, Tea	$2.00
Rice	$1.25	Shake	$2.75

_____

Chocolate cake	$5.25
Vanilla ice cream	$2.75
Cheesecake	$4.75

C Discuss with a partner which food group each item is in.

D Put the following conversation in the correct order.
Write the correct number next to each line

____ _Server:_ What do you want to drink?
____ _Customer:_ That's all, thank you.
____ _Customer:_ Yes, I'll have the steak and a baked potato, please.

____ _Customer:_ Mineral water, please.
_1_ _Server:_ Can I take your order?
____ _Server:_ Anything else?

E Make groups of three students. Two of you are customers, and one is a server. Make similar conversations, using the food from the menu.

Planning a menu

1. Form a team with four or five students. You are a family of four or five people. You only have $150.00 for food for the next week. What can you make for breakfast, lunch, and dinner? Make a menu and go shopping.

Position	Job	Student Name
Student 1 Team leader	See that everyone speaks English. See that everyone participates.	
Student 2	You cook the food for the family.	
Student 3	You do the shopping for the family.	
Student 4	Prepare a class presentation with help from the team.	

2. Choose a name for your family.

3. Fill in a calendar with your food for breakfast, lunch, and dinner for one week. (See pages 53 and 54.)

4. Make a shopping list. How much of each item do you need? Work out the prices. Make sure the total is under $150.

5. Make a family presentation to the class. Tell the class about the meals on your menu. How much money did you spend? How much money is left? What can you do with the money that is left over?

Dairy		**Meat, Fish, Beans**		**Fruits**	
Milk	$3.09 a gallon	Hamburger	$2.99 a pound	Bananas	$1.29 a pound
Eggs	$1.59 a dozen	Chicken	$.99 a pound	Oranges	$.49 a pound
Grains		Fish	$4.99 a pound	**Snacks**	
Bread	$2.39 a loaf	Tuna fish	$1.29 a can	Cookies	$2.59 a box
Cereal	$2.39 a box	Peanut butter	$2.39 a jar	Pretzels	$1.69 a bag
Pasta	$1.19 a box	**Vegetables**			
Beans	$1.59 a can	Tomatoes	$1.59 a pound		
Oils		Lettuce	$1.29 a head		
Olive oil	$2.99 a bottle	Potatoes	$.69 a pound		
		Broccoli	$1.19 a head		

PRONUNCIATION

Which syllable is stressed? Listen and mark the stressed syllables.

· ● ·	· ● ·	● ·
tomato	spaghetti	yogurt
banana	calendar	breakfast
broccoli	nutrition	dessert

LEARNER LOG

Circle what you learned and write the page number where you learned it.

1. I know words for food.
   Yes Maybe No   Page _____

2. I can read a menu.
   Yes Maybe No   Page _____

3. I can ask for directions in a market.
   Yes Maybe No   Page _____

4. I can talk about containers and quantity.
   Yes Maybe No   Page _____

5. I know about food groups.
   Yes Maybe No   Page _____

6. I can plan a healthy meal.
   Yes Maybe No   Page _____

7. I can use the simple present.
   Yes Maybe No   Page _____

8. I can order food in a restaurant.
   Yes Maybe No   Page _____

Did you answer *No?* Review the information with a partner.

Rank what you like to do best from 1–6. 1 is your favorite activity. Your teacher will help you.

☐ practice listening

☐ practice speaking

☐ practice reading

☐ practice writing

☐ learn grammar

☐ learn new words (vocabulary)

In the next unit, I want to focus on

_____.

GOALS

- Identify types of housing
- Talk about bank accounts
- Combine sentences
- Scan for information
- Fill out a rental application
- Identify furniture in a house
- Describe locations

LESSON **1** Finding a place to live

GOAL ▶ Identify types of housing | *Vocabulary*

Who are the people in the picture?
Where are they from?
What kind of house do they live in?

A **Listen to the story with your book closed.**
Then read the story and answer the questions.

My name is Kyung. My family and I moved from Korea to Arcadia, Florida last month. I have a good job here in Arcadia, but we need to find a place to live. We are living with friends right now in a small house. We need to find a house or apartment, buy furniture, and open a bank account. We have a lot to do.

1. Where is Kyung from? _____

2. Where does he work? _____

3. Where is he living now? _____

4. What does he need to do? _____

B Read the advertisements. Draw a line from the advertisement to the correct picture.

Three-bedroom house to rent
$1200 per month,
315 Madison St.

Three-bedroom mobile home
Rent $750 a month,
1700 Grove St.

Three-bedroom apartment—
Rent $700 a month,
2200 Atlantic Ave. #211

Three-bedroom condominium
to buy $85,000,
12 Shady Glen

C Ask a partner questions about the price of housing.

EXAMPLE:
Student A: How much is the house on Madison Street?
Student B: It's $1200 a month to rent.

D Do a housing survey. Talk to four students and fill in the chart.

EXAMPLE:
Student A: What kind of housing do you live in?
Student B: I live in a mobile home.

Student A: Do you want to move?
Student B: Yes, I want to buy a condominium.

Name	. . . lives in a . . .	. . . wants to live in a . . .

LESSON 2 Opening a bank account

GOAL ▶ **Talk about bank accounts**

 Life Skill

A **Use the words in the box to talk about the pictures.**

write a check	bank teller	take out money	PIN number
ATM	ATM card	deposit money	photo ID

B **Kyung needs a bank account before he can rent a home. What does he need to open a bank account? Listen to his conversation at the bank. Circle the correct answer.**

Kyung wants a savings account and a checking account.	True	False
He can write checks from a savings account.	True	False
He needs two kinds of ID to open a bank account.	True	False
He needs to deposit money to open an account.	True	False
He can get his checks immediately.	True	False

Kyung uses checks to pay for food and other things. He writes down all his deposits and payments in a check ledger. Read the information and fill in the missing totals.

Check #	Date	Description	Payment (−)	Deposit (+)	Balance	
	July 2	First deposit		800.00	800	00
001	July 10	Renco Market	87.57		−87	57
					712	43
002	July 12	Sal's Clothes	37.50			
	July 12	Paycheck		622.54		
003	July 17	Renco Market	105.33			

D How much is the check for? What did Kyung buy with this check?

Kyung Kim   #001

Date *July 10, 2003*

Pay to the order of ___*Renco Market*_____ | $ | 87.57

___*eighty-seven dollars and* --------------57/100_____ Dollars

Family Bank of Florida

For ___*food*_____   *Kyung Kim*_____

:011000111 : 005 0000 00X0

Think about your budget each week. Fill in the amounts below.

How much do you pay for food each month? $_____ (Check # 0035)
How much do you pay for clothing each month? $_____ (Check # 0036)
How much do you pay for your phone each month? $_____ (Check # 0037)

F **Complete the check ledger with your information.**

Check #	Date	Description	Payment (−)	Deposit (+)	Balance	
					$800	
0035						
0036						
0037						

G **Fill in the correct information on the check.**

Your Name   #0035

                                              Date _____

Pay to the
order of _____ $ [   ]

_____ Dollars

Your Bank's Name

For _____   _____

: 011000XXX : 00X 0000 0000

LESSON 3 **Describing a home**

GOAL ▶ **Combine sentences**   *Grammar*

A Write the names of the rooms on the key.

yard	bedroom	bathroom
kitchen	dining room	living room

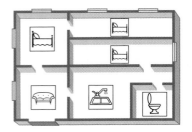   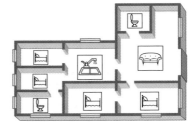   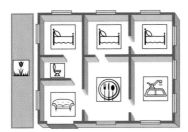

Plan 1: $1400   Plan 2: $2000 NEW   Plan 3: $1400

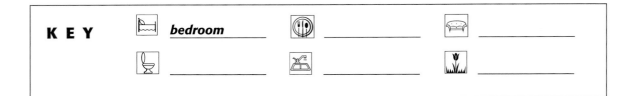

K E Y   🛏 *bedroom* _____   ⊞ _____   🛋 _____

🚽 _____   🔥 _____   🌱 _____

B Read.

Now that Kyung has a bank account, he needs a home. He wants to rent a three-bedroom house. Here are the floor plans of three different houses. What is the same about these floor plans? What is different?

C Complete the sentences using the information above.

1. Plan 2 **has four bedrooms. It's $2000 a month.** _____

2. Plan 3 **has** _____

3. Plans 1 and 3 **have one bathroom. They are $1400 a month.** _____

4. Plans 2 and 3 _____

Study the charts with your teacher.

Combining sentences				
Subject			Subject	
Plan 2	<u>has</u> four bedrooms.		It	<u>is</u> $2000 a month.
Plan 2	<u>has</u> four bedrooms	**and**	**it**	<u>is</u> $2000 a month.
Plan 2 has four bedrooms and it's $2000 a month.				

Combining sentences				
Subject			Subject	
Plans 1 and 3	<u>have</u> one bathroom.		They	<u>are</u> $1400 a month.
Plans 1 and 3	<u>have</u> one bathroom	**and**	**t**hey	<u>are</u> $1400 a month.
Plans 1 and 3 have one bathroom and they are $1400 a month.				

E **Look at the sentences about floor plans from page 66. Combine sentences.**

EXAMPLE: Plan 2 has four bedrooms. It is $2000 a month.
Plan 2 has four bedrooms and it's $2000 a month.

1. Plans 1 and 3 have three bedrooms. They are $1400 a month.

   _____

2. Plans 1 and 3 have one bathroom. They have small living rooms.

   _____

3. Plan 2 has a large living room. It has two bathrooms.

   _____

4. Plan 3 has a yard. It isn't new.

   _____

F **Write two sentences about your home. Then combine the sentences using *and*.**

Sentence 1: _____

Sentence 2: _____

Combined sentence: _____

GOAL ▶ Scan for information

A Talk in groups about your home.

1. Do you live in a house, an apartment, or a condominium?
2. How many bedrooms are in your home?
3. Is your home large or small?
4. Is your home one-story or two?
5. Do you have a yard or a balcony?
6. Is your home old or new?

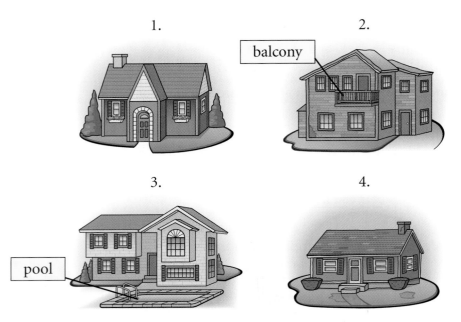

1.

balcony

2.

3.

pool

4.

B Match the number of the picture with the correct description below.

____ This large four-bedroom house is the perfect rental for big families. The house is old but in very good condition. The neighborhood is quiet but comfortable. There is a beautiful view from the balcony. This two-story house rents for $1500 a month and utilities are included.

__*1*__ Come and see this new, small, one-story dream house. It is in a small, friendly neighborhood. This house rents for only $700 a month. It has one bedroom and a large kitchen. You will love it when you see it.

____ Sometimes older is better. This small two-bedroom house has an interesting history. The same person has owned it for 50 years. Yard needs work. Rent it for an amazing $600 a month.

____ If you want to rent a big home and money is not important, rent this very large five-bedroom house with swimming pool. It's great value for only $2500 a month.

HOUSING FOR RENT

1. **For Rent:** 2 bdrm, 2bath, condo, ac, utils paid, nr park and schools, Daily City, $650.00, call 555-7677

2. **For Rent:** 1 bdrm, 1bath apt, new carpet, Sycamore St. Costa Mesa, $625

3. **For Rent:** 4 bdrm, 3 bath, hse, pool, frpl, balcony, Luxury Heights, $950, lease only, 5253 Bountiful St. Come and see!

4. **For Rent:** 3 bdrm, 1 bath condo, ac, water pd, good community, nr shopping, 555-3232 in Bridgemont

5. **For Rent:** 3 bdrm apt, $500, cln, AC, no pets, new refr. incl. Tustin, 555-3722

6. **For Rent:** 2 bdrm mobile home, utils pd., $700, like new, Seawall Estates, Newton, call 555-3511

C **Look at the housing ads and answer the questions.**

1. Which ads are under $600 a month?

_____

2. Which ads have air conditioning?

_____

3. Which ad has a new refrigerator?

_____

4. Which ad has 3 bathrooms?

_____

D **Review the vocabulary with your teacher. Can you find the abbreviations in the ads above?**

Vocabulary	Abbreviations	Vocabulary	Abbreviations
bedroom	*bdrm*	air conditioning	
condominium	*condo*	house	
utilities		paid	
near		included	
bathroom		refrigerator	
apartment		fireplace	

E **In a group, write a classified ad. Answer these questions in your ad.**

1. How much is the rent?
2. How many bedrooms?
3. How many bathrooms?
4. Who do you call?
5. What's the phone number?

  Active Task: Find examples of housing ads in a newspaper or on the Internet.

GOAL ▶ Fill out a rental application

Kyung is looking for a home.
He looked in the classified ads and now he is
talking to a rental agent.

 A **Listen to the conversation. What are Kyung's needs and what are his wants? Complete the chart.**

Needs	Wants
Three-bedroom house	Near school
Under $900	

For Rent:
2 bdrm, 2 bath, hse, utils pd, big yard, nr schools, $1050, call Janet at 555-2425

1.

For Rent
3 bdrm two story house, garage, ac, nr schools and shopping, $1500, call 555-3534

2.

For Rent: 3 bdrm, 2 bath apt, utils pd, no deposit, big living room, nr schools, small yard, separate garage, $750 a month lease or rent, call 555-6565

3.

FOR RENT:
4 bdroom, 3 bath condo, nr schools, big yard, no pets, one story, $925, call Rick at **555-6789**

4.

B **In groups, talk about which home is good for Kyung.**

Look at the application form and answer the questions.

1. What is Kyung's address now?

   _____

2. What was his address before he came to Florida?

   _____

3. What is the name of the company where he works?

   _____

4. What is Kyung's wife's name?

   _____

5. What is her job?

   _____

RENTAL APPLICATION FORM

Applicant: *Kyung Kim*
Interviewed by: *Paula Wharton*
Present Address: *33457 Akron St., Arcadia, Florida 34265*
Phone: *555- 5059*
Prior Address: *134-2 Chongun-Dong, Chongno-Ku Seoul Korea*
Landlord: *Fred Wharton*
Prior Landlord: *NA*
Employer: *Sift Manufacturing*
Position: *Computer Technician*
Personal Reference: *James Baker, Manuel Acevedo*
Relationship: *Boss, Supervisor*
References:

Co- Applicant or Spouse: *Nam- young Kim*
Employer: *Roscoe Metals*
Position: *Assembly Worker*
Personal Reference: *George Pratt*
Relationship: *Supervisor*

Bank Information:
Name of Bank: *Family Bank of Florida*
Checking Account No.: *011000111 005 0000 0000*
Savings Account No.: *0X0000 000XX*

 Fill out the rental application above with your information.

RENTAL APPLICATION FORM
Applicant:
Interviewed by:
Present Address:
Phone:
Prior Address:
Landlord:
Prior Landlord:
Employer:
Position:
Personal Reference:
Relationship:
References:

Co- Applicant or Spouse:
Employer:
Position:
Personal Reference:
Relationship:

Bank Information:
Name of Bank:
Checking Account No.:
Savings Account No.:

LESSON 6 Choosing furniture for your home

GOAL ▶ **Identify furniture in a house**

Vocabulary

A Kyung is ready to rent a home. Read about the home he rents.

RENTAL PROPERTY:

3 bdrm, 2 bath apt, utils pd, no deposit, big living room, nr schools, small yard, separate garage, new remodeled kitchen, new washer/dryer, dishwasher, stove and oven, $750 a month rent or lease, call 555-6565

How many bedrooms and bathrooms does it have?
How much is the rent?
What is nearby?

B Match the words with the correct pictures.

stove	washer/dryer	microwave
	dishwasher	refrigerator

_____ _____ _____ _____ _____

C What else do you have in the kitchen? Write the names here and draw a picture for each one.

_____ _____ _____ _____

sofa   lamp   chair   bed   armchair

dresser   dining room set   bookcase (bookshelves)   coffee table   wardrobe

D **Kyung needs to buy furniture for his new home. Help him decide what he needs. Write the words in the floor plan.**

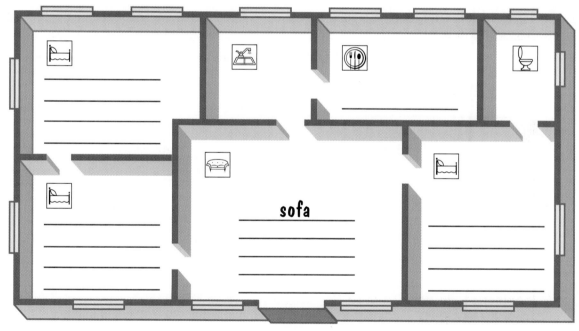

sofa

E **Practice the conversation with a partner. Make similar conversations using the furniture on the floor plan.**

EXAMPLE:
Student A: What does Kyung need?
Student B: He needs one <u>sofa</u> for the living room.
Student A: What does he need for the bedrooms?
Student B: He needs <u>three beds</u> for the bedrooms.

F Complete the invoice. How much furniture does Kyung need?

McCarthy's Furniture Warehouse				
Quantity	Merchandise	Unit Price	Total	
1	sofa	$850.89	$850	89
	armchair	$449.99		
	end table	$125.89		
	coffee table	$375.99		
	lamp	$29.49		
	dining room set	$575.00		
3	bed	$425.75		
	wardrobe	$279.99		
	dresser	$269.89		
Subtotal				
Total				

G How much furniture do you need for your home? Complete the invoice.

McCarthy's Furniture Warehouse				
Quantity	Merchandise	Unit Price	Total	
	sofa	$850.89		
	armchair	$449.99		
	end table	$125.89		
	coffee table	$375.99		
	lamp	$29.49		
	dining room set	$575.00		
	bed	$425.75		
	wardrobe	$279.99		
	dresser	$269.89		
Subtotal				
Total				

H Talk to a partner about what you need.

EXAMPLE: I need one sofa at $850.89.

I **Active Task:** Find the prices of these furniture items at a store or on the Internet and tell the class.

GOAL ▶ **Describe locations**

Kyung and his family are
    moving in.
Kyung's wife Nam-young is
    telling the others where to
    put the furniture.

A **Listen to the conversation and complete the chart.**

Items	Location
table	in the corner
	under the sink
	on the kitchen counter
	over the refrigerator

B **What did Nam-young say?**

1. *Put the table in the corner.* _____
2. _____
3. _____
4. _____

C **Study the chart with your teacher.**

	Prepositions of location
	The dishes are <u>in</u> the cupboard.
	The bananas are <u>on</u> the kitchen counter.
	The picture is <u>over</u> the refrigerator.
	The soap is <u>under</u> the sink.
	The microwave is <u>between</u> the toaster and the refrigerator.
	The box is <u>in the corner</u>.
	The nightstand is <u>next to</u> the bed.
	The vacuum cleaner is <u>in front of</u> the dishwasher.
	The yard is <u>in back of</u> the house.

D **Use the prepositions from the chart to describe the picture.**

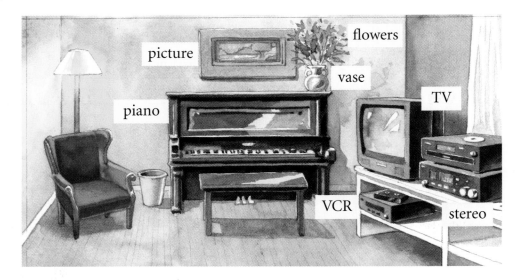

E **Describe a room in your home. Use the words from this lesson. Your partner will listen and draw a picture of your room.**

Review

A Use the information from the ad to match the questions and the answers. Write the correct letter next to each question.

1. How many bedrooms does it have? _____

2. Is it near the shopping mall? _____

3. How much is the rent? _____

4. Are utilities included? _____

a. No, it is near the schools.

b. $650 a month.

c. Yes, electricity and gas and water are included.

d. It has two bedrooms.

B Complete the chart using the information above.

Size	Location	Cost
2 bedrooms		Utilities are paid
	Downtown Santa Ana	

C Now combine the information from each section to make a sentence using *and*.

EXAMPLE:

Size: ***The apartment has two bedrooms and it has one bathroom.***

Location: _____

Cost: _____

D You want to rent this apartment from Mr. Gallart. Write a check for the first month's rent.

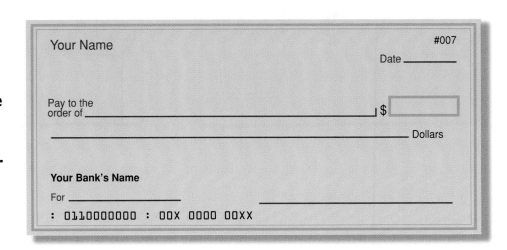

 E   **Look at the picture and complete the sentences.**

1. The TV is _____ the table.

2. The picture is _____ the desk.

3. The flowers are _____ the TV.

4. The window is _____ the sofa.

5. The table is _____ the corner.

6. The books are _____ the table.

7. The armchair is _____ the desk.

8. The lamp is _____ the armchair and the TV.

F   **Draw the following items on the picture. Then describe your picture to your partner.**

| microwave | toaster | dishes | trash can | dishwasher | refrigerator | stove |

Draw your kitchen here.

Draw your partner's kitchen here.

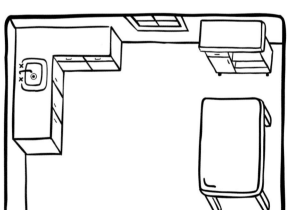

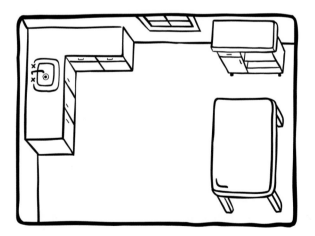

T E A M
PROJECT

Planning a move

1. Form a team with four or five students. Your group will be a family who is going to move. In a family group, make a plan to move.

   In your team, you need:

Position	Job	Student Name
Student 1 Team Leader	See that everyone speaks English. See that everyone participates.	
Student 2 Finance Planner	Plan to pay rent and buy furniture with help from the team.	
Student 3 Secretary	Fill out a rental application with help from the team.	
Student 4 Decorator	Put furniture in the home with help from the team.	

2. Describe your family and your new home. (See page 68.)
   - How many bedrooms do you need?
   - What kind of home do you need (house, condo, apartment)?
   - How much money can you pay for rent?
   - Write a classified ad about the home you want. (See page 69.)

3. Make a list of the furniture you need. (See pages 73–74.)

4. Fill out an invoice for furniture and write a check for the furniture. (See pages 64 and 74.)

5. Fill out a rental application. (See page 71.)

6. Make a floor plan of the home and add furniture. (See page 73.)

7. Report to the class. Show the floor plan and read the classified ad.

PRONUNCIATION

Listen to the intonation and repeat each question. Add arrows to questions 3 and 4. Make up your own example for question 5.

1. Is the house old or new?

2. Is the dining room large or small?

3. Is the rent expensive or cheap?

4. Is the apartment noisy or quiet?

5. _____ ?

LEARNER LOG

Circle what you learned and write the page number where you learned it.

1. I know about different kinds of housing.
   Yes   Maybe   No   Page _____

2. I can open a checking account.
   Yes   Maybe   No   Page _____

3. I can balance a check ledger.
   Yes   Maybe   No   Page _____

4. I can describe rooms in a house.
   Yes   Maybe   No   Page _____

5. I can fill out a rental application.
   Yes   Maybe   No   Page _____

6. I can make a compound sentence.
   Yes   Maybe   No   Page _____

7. I can use prepositions of location.
   Yes   Maybe   No   Page _____

Did you answer *No?* Review the information with a partner.

Rank what you like to do best from 1 to 6. 1 is your favorite activity. Your teacher will help you.

☐ practice listening

☐ practice speaking

☐ practice reading

☐ practice writing

☐ learn grammar

☐ learn new words (vocabulary)

In the next unit, I want to focus on

_____.

Our Community

GOALS

- Describe a neighborhood
- Identify buildings
- Use prepositions to describe location

- Follow directions
- Read a directory index
- Use simple present and present continuous
- Send a letter

  **Getting around town**

GOAL ▶ Describe a neighborhood   *Vocabulary*

A **Read the paragraph.**

Palm City is a small community. The homes and schools are all in the northwest. There is a mall with 100 stores in the northeast. In the southeast there is a big entertainment center with a bowling alley, movie theaters, a miniature golf course and many other kinds of entertainment. There are factories and companies in the southwest part of the town. The bus circles the city in exactly one hour.

B **Look at the chart. Read the story about the community again and fill in the missing words below.**

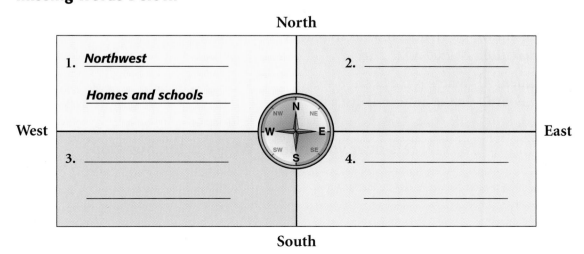

North

1. *Northwest*

  Homes and schools

2. _____

  _____

West

3. _____

  _____

4. _____

  _____

East

South

C Look at the bus schedule. Write the names of the streets on the map.

PALM CITY
BUS SERVICE—
MORNING SCHEDULE

Residential area
Radcliff and Main St.

7:00
8:00
9:00
10:00

Shopping mall
Broadway and Manchester

7:15
8:15
9:15
10:15

Entertainment center
First and Main St.

7:30
8:30
9:30
10:30

Industrial district
Broadway and Commonwealth

7:45
8:45
9:45
10:45

D Ask a partner questions about the schedule.

EXAMPLES:
Student A: When does the bus stop in the residential area?
Student B: At 7:00 A.M.

Student A: Where is the bus at 8:45?
Student B: In the industrial district.

E What are four streets near your home? Where is the bus stop?

LESSON 2 — Where's the supermarket?

GOAL ▶ **Identify buildings**

Vocabulary

A Study these words with your teacher. What can you buy or do in each place?

~~Apartment~~	Department store	House	Police station
Bank	Fast food restaurant	Library	Post office
~~City Hall~~	Fire station	Mall	Restaurant
~~Clothes store~~	Gas station	Mobile home	Shoe store
Condominium	Hardware store	Pet store	Supermarket
Courthouse	Hospital	Pharmacy	

B Write the words above in the correct category below. What other words can you add to each category?

Residential	Public and Service	Buy and Sell

Apartment	*City Hall*	*Clothes store*
Condominium	Fire station	supermarket
Mall		shoe store
Mobile home	Hospital	supermarket
	Bank	pet store
	Library	Restaurant
	police station	Department stor
		Gas St
	Post office	Hard ware stor
	court house	Gas station
		Pharmacy

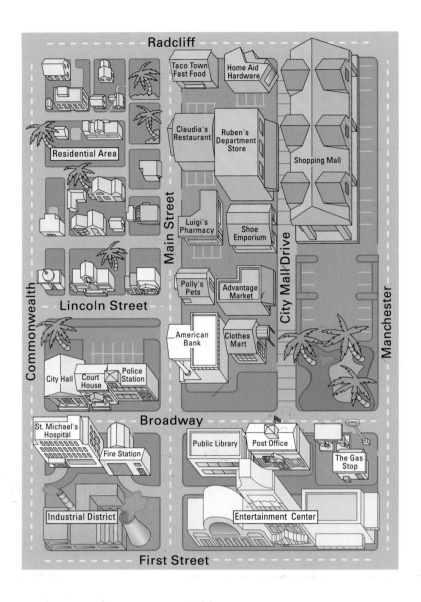

C **Practice the conversation with a partner. Use the place names from the map.**

EXAMPLE:
Student A: Excuse me. Where's <u>Advantage Market</u>?
Student B: It's on <u>City Mall Drive</u> next to the <u>Shoe Emporium</u>.
Student A: Thank you.

D **What are the names of stores in your community? Make a list on another piece of paper.**

E **Active Task:** Find a map of your neighborhood and show your partner where you usually shop.

LESSON 3 It's next to the library.

GOAL ▶ **Use prepositions to describe location**   *Grammar*

 A **Study the prepositions below. You can use them to describe location.**

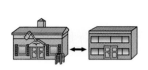 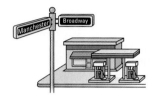 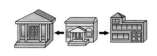 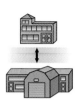

The post office is **next to** the library.

The gas station is **on the corner of** Broadway and Manchester.

The courthouse is **between** City Hall and the police station.

The police station is **across from** the fire station.

 B **Look at the map on page 84. Write the prepositions *between, next to, on the corner of, across from.***

1. Clothes Mart is _____ Advantage Market.

2. Shoe Emporium is _____ the mall.

3. Taco Town is _____ Radcliff and Main.

4. Advantage Market is _____ Shoe Emporium and Clothes Mart.

5. The fire station is _____ St. Michael's Hospital.

6. The courthouse is _____ St. Michael's Hospital.

7. Claudia's Restaurant is _____ Luigi's Pharmacy and Taco Town.

8. Home Aid Hardware is _____ Radcliff and City Mall Drive.

 C **Work in pairs. Ask and answer three questions about the locations in exercise B. Student A looks only on this page. Student B looks only on page 84. Then change roles.**

EXAMPLE:
Student A: Where's Clothes Mart?
Student B: Clothes Mart is next to Advantage Market.

Read the letter. Underline prepositions of location.

February 10
Dear Raquel,

How are you? I'm fine and happy. I'm writing this letter in English for practice. I miss Haiti but I have a new job in Palm City now and I really like it. I work at the hospital. The hospital is across from the City Hall and the courthouse. Sometimes I have to go to the City Hall to deliver birth certificates.

Palm City is a nice community. There is a park on the corner near the hospital where I eat my lunch. It's beautiful outside almost every day. Sometimes I eat dinner at a restaurant around the corner from my apartment on Main Street. The restaurant is good but Taco Town next to Claudia's Restaurant is faster and I eat there when I'm in a hurry.

I am drawing a map of Palm City so you can see it. I'm also mailing pictures for you. I hope you can visit me soon.

Your friend,
Marie

E **Answer the questions in sentences. Use prepositions.**

1. Where does Marie eat lunch?

   She eats lunch in the park.   *It's on the corner near the hospital.*

2. Where does Marie work? Where is the building?

   She works at the hospital.   *It's_____.*

3. Where does she usually eat dinner? Where is the building?

   She eats at_____.   *It's_____.*

4. Where does she eat when she is in a hurry?

   She eats at_____.   *It's_____.*

F **Write sentences about your community on another sheet of paper.**

Finding your way

GOAL ▶ **Follow directions**

What is Raquel doing?
Who is she talking to?

A **Listen to the conversation with your book closed. Then listen and read.**

Marie: Hello.
Raquel: Hi, Marie. I'm here!
Marie: Where?
Raquel: Here in Palm City.
Marie: Really? Where are you right now?
Raquel: I'm at the intersection of Main and Lincoln.
Marie: Wow, that's great. You can walk here! Go north on Main. Walk straight ahead for three blocks and turn left on Fairview. Go one block and turn right. Turn left on Washington. My apartment is on the right at 133 Washington #15.

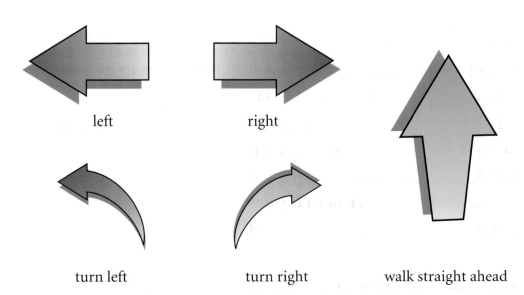

left   right

turn left   turn right   walk straight ahead

B **Practice the conversation with a partner.**

C Listen to the conversation again and draw Raquel's route to Marie's apartment on the map.

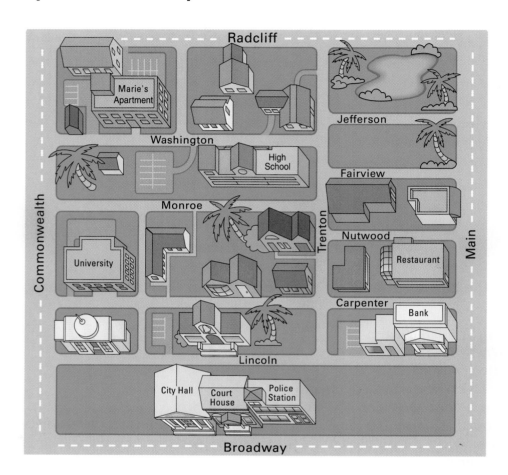

D. **Work in pairs. Student A, look at this page. Student B, look at page 89. Student A, give these directions to your partner. Your partner will find and label these locations on the map on page 89. Then listen to your partner's directions.**

You say:

1. You are at the intersection of Broadway and Main. Find the high school. Go north on Main four blocks and turn left. Go one block and turn right. Then turn left and it's on the left.

2. You are at the intersection of Commonwealth and Monroe. Find the bank. Go east on Monroe for two blocks. Turn right on Trenton and go two blocks. Then turn left, it's at the end of the block on the corner.

3. You are at the intersection of Lincoln and Trenton. Find the restaurant. Go north on Trenton two blocks and turn right. It's on the right at the end of the block.

4. You are at the intersection of Radcliff and Main. Find the university. _____

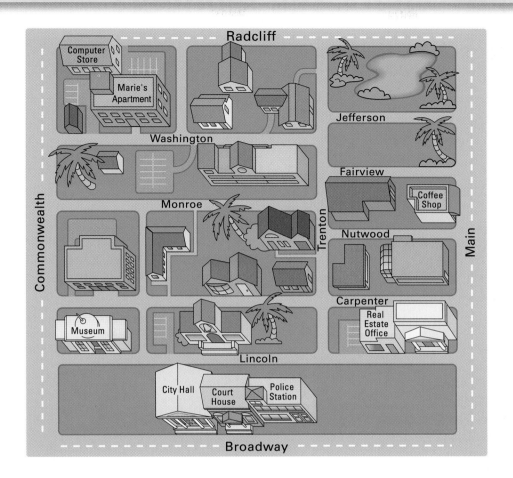

E **Student B, look at this page. First listen to Student A's directions. Then give these directions to your partner. Your partner will find and label these locations on the map on page 88.**

You say:

1. You are at the intersection of Broadway and Main. Find the museum. Go north on Main one block and turn left. Go three blocks and it's on the right.

2. You are at the intersection of Carpenter and Commonwealth. Find the real estate office. Go east on Carpenter two blocks and turn right. Go one block and turn left. It's on the left.

3. You are at the intersection of Fairview and Trenton. Find the computer store. Go north on Trenton and turn left on Washington. Walk straight ahead one block and turn right. Then turn left and it's on the left.

4. You are at the intersection of Commonwealth and Radcliff. Find the coffee shop. _____

_____

F **Active Task:** Bring a street map or a map from the Internet and mark the path to your home from the nearest train or bus station.

GOAL ▶ **Read a directory index**

Palm City Local Phone Directory Index

Art Galleries...8	Hospital 27
Attorneys 9-12	Lawyers– See Attorneys
Banks 12-13	Museums 27
Churches 13-17	Optometrists 27-28
Clothes– Retail 17-21	Physicians 28
Community Services iv	Real Estate Agencies 29
Libraries (public)	Rental Cars 29-30
Playgrounds and Parks	Restaurants 30-32
Dentists..21	Schools (private) 32
Department Stores 22-23	Schools (public) 32
Doctors– See physicians, optometrists,	Shoes– Retail 32-33
dentists	Supermarkets– See grocers
Fast Food– See Restaurants	Transportation 33-35
Furniture– Retail 24	Bus Lines
Government– See white pages	Car Rental
Grocers and Markets 24-25	Shuttle Service
Home Improvement 25-26	Train
	Taxis
	Travel Agencies 35

> Marie is at work and Raquel need to call for information

A Scan the index and find the page numbers.

Page

24–25   Raquel wants to go to the market.

_____   Raquel needs a new dress.

_____   Raquel needs a car for a week.

_____   Raquel wants to take Marie to a nice restaurant.

_____   Raquel wants to call Marie at work.

City Hall	555-3300	Police Department	555-4867
160 W. Broadway		Emergencies call 911	
Courthouse	555-5245	140 Broadway	
150 W. Broadway			
DMV (Department of Motor Vehicles)		Schools (Public)	
Information	555-2227	Jefferson Middle	555-2665
Appointments		122 Jefferson St.	
375 Western Ave.	555-2778	Lincoln High	555-8336
Fire Department	555-3473	278 Lincoln Ave.	
Emergencies call 911		Washington Elementary	555-5437
145 W. Broadway		210 Washington St.	
Library (Public)	555-7323		
125 E. Broadway		U.S. Post Office	555-6245
Playgrounds and Parks		151 E. Broadway	
Department of Parks			
and Recreation			
160 W. Broadway,			
Suite 15	555-7275		
Angel Park			
137 Monroe St.	555-3224		
Lilly Community Park			
275 Carpenter	555-2211		

> Marie has important numbers by her phone. Where can Raquel go to find books to read?

B Ask a partner for the address and telephone number of the post office, courthouse, DMV, Jefferson Middle School, fire department, and City Hall.

EXAMPLE: ***Student A:*** Where's the post office?
Student B: It's at 151 E. Broadway.
Student A: Thank you. What's the telephone number?
Student B: It's 555-6245.

C Cover the list and listen to the phone conversations. Write the places, addresses, and phone numbers you hear in the chart.

Place	Address	Phone
Ex. post office	151 E. Broadway	555–6245
1.		
2.		
3.		
4.		

Waiting for Marie

GOAL ▶ **Use simple present and present continuous**   *Grammar*

 A **Close your book and listen. Then read Raquel's postcard.**

What is Raquel doing?
Who do you think Antonio is?

March 5

Dear Antonio,

    I am writing to you from Palm City in California. I am staying here for a few days with my friend Marie. I am having a wonderful time. Palm City is beautiful. People are very friendly. Sometimes we go to Claudia's Restaurant to eat Mexican food. It's great.

    Marie works in the hospital here as a nurse. She goes to work early every day and she works very hard. She loves her new job, but she is a little sad because her family and friends aren't here.

    Right now I am doing my English homework and listening to music at Marie's house. I am waiting for Marie to finish work. See you soon.

            Love,

             Raquel

Antonio Sanchez
3450 Av. São João
21525-060
Rio de Janeiro-RJ
BRAZIL

B **Answer the questions.**

1. Is Raquel happy or sad? _____

2. What is Raquel doing right now? _____

3. What does Marie do every day? _____

4. Is Marie happy or sad? _____

Put the sentences from the postcard on page 92 in the charts.

Simple present	
be verb	Other verbs
Palm City is beautiful.	Sometimes we go to Claudia's Restaurant to eat.

Present continuous
I am writing to you from Palm City.

D **Complete the sentences with the simple present or the present continuous.**

EXAMPLE:
The people _____**are**_____ (be) friendly.

1. Palm City _____ (be) a small city.

2. Antonio _____ (wait) for a letter right now.

3. Raquel never _____ (work) at the hospital.

4. At this moment, Raquel _____ (eat) lunch.

5. Marie _____ (go) to school two days a week.

E **Write sentences about you and your city.**

Simple present	
be verb	Other verbs
I am an English student.	(I never) I never watch TV.
My city is	(I rarely) I rarely eat ice cream.
	(Sometimes I)
	(I often)
	(I always)

F **What are you doing right now?**

Present continuous
I'm writing in my book.

G **Ask your partner what he or she does and what he or she is doing. Write sentences about your partner.**

1. He/She never _____
2. At this moment he/she _____
3. He/She rarely _____
4. Sometimes he/she _____
5. Right now he/she _____
6. He/She always _____
7. Right now he/she _____
8. At this moment he/she _____

GOAL ▶ Send a letter

A Read the parts of the letter and put them in the correct order. Write the correct number next to each part.

a._____   I am sending you a package with a gift for you.

b._1_   March 12

c._____   This city is wonderful. The weather is warm most of the time. There are many parks, stores, and restaurants. There is good bus service. The bus goes around the city in an hour and stops near the shopping mall. The shopping mall has over a hundred stores and I go there every day. The parks are very beautiful. There are a lot of palm trees and cactus plants.

d._____   Dear Antonio,

e._____   Raquel

f._____   I am writing to tell you that I am staying with Marie in Palm City for one more week. I am having a lot of fun. Marie is very nice and kind. She likes to go shopping and she eats at fast-food restaurants a lot. We walk in the park every day on her lunch break.

g._____   Love always,

B Look at the envelope for Raquel's letter.

Raquel Jobim
133 Washington Street #15
Palm City, CA 92777

        Antonio Sanchez
        3450 Av. São João
        21525-060
        Rio de Janeiro-RJ
        BRAZIL

C Listen to the conversation with your book closed. Then read the conversation with a partner.

Where is Raquel?
What is she doing?

Raquel: I want to send this letter and package to Brazil, please.

Clerk: The letter is 80 cents. Do you want the package insured?

Raquel: No, thank you. I don't need insurance.

Clerk: You need to fill in a customs form.

Raquel: Yes, here it is.

Clerk: Do you want this to go airmail or economy?

Raquel: Airmail, please.

Clerk: OK, then the total is $17.80.

Raquel: Thank you.

D Discuss the questions with your class.

1. What is insurance?

2. What information do you need to write on a customs form?

3. Does it cost more for airmail or economy?

4. How much is the package?

E Ask a friend for his or her address. Complete the envelope. Use your own address for the return address.

F **Active Task:** Go to a post office and find out about the cost of sending a one-pound package to your friend or family. Tell the class what you find out.

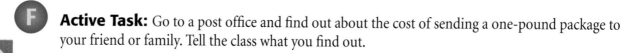

Review

A Read the directions and follow the route on the map. Write the name of the place where you arrive.

| post office | hospital | bank | library | pharmacy |

1. You are at the intersection of Montgomery and Vallejo. Go west on Vallejo for three blocks and turn left. Go one block. It's on the right. _____

2. You are at the intersection of Chestnut and Powell. Go south on Powell for one block. Then go west on Lombard one block. It's across the street. _____

3. You are at the intersection of Broadway and Powell. Go south on Powell. Go two blocks and turn left. It's on the right. _____

4. You are at the intersection of Union and Mason. Go east on Union for two blocks. Then turn left. It's on the right. _____

5. You are at the intersection of Green and Mason. Go west on Green for four blocks. Then go north one block. It's on the corner. _____

Review

B **Write the names of the places where you can do these things.**

1. Send a package by airmail. _____
2. Borrow a book. _____
3. Buy gas for your car. _____
4. Buy medicine. _____
5. Eat a burger and french fries. _____
6. Find a doctor. _____
7. Report a crime. _____
8. Register the birth of a new baby. _____

C **Read the description and fill in the blanks with the correct form of the verb *be*.**

This city _____ wonderful. The weather _____ warm most of the time. There _____ many parks, stores, and restaurants. There _____ a good bus service. The bus goes around the city in an hour and stops near the shopping mall. There _____ over a hundred stores in the shopping mall and I go there every day. The parks _____ very beautiful. There _____ a lot of palm trees and beautiful flowers.

D **Read the letter and underline the correct verb forms.**

Dear Roberto,

I write/am writing to you from California. I sit/am sitting on the beach. I stay/am staying here in Santa Barbara with my friend Suzanna. It's very warm and sunny. We walk/are walking on the beach every day. We often eat/are eating Mexican food in the evening. On weekends we visit/are visiting beautiful places along the coast.

Is it warm in Texas right now? I hope you have/are having a nice holiday there.

Your friend,

Sara

T E A M PROJECT

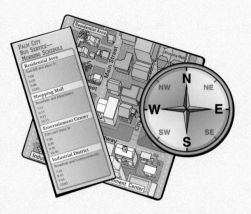

Describing your community

1. Form a team with four or five students. In a group you are going to describe your community and send a letter to a friend.

   In your team, you need:

Position	Job	Student Name
Student 1 Leader	See that everyone speaks English. See that everyone participates.	
Student 2 Secretary	Write a paragraph about your community with help from the team.	
Student 3 Artist and designer	Make a map of the community with help from the team.	
Student 4 Spokesperson(s)	Prepare a group presentation with help from the team.	

2. Draw a map of the community around your school. (See pages 88 and 89.)
   • What buildings are there?
   • What are the names of the streets?
   • Is there a city bus? Where does it stop?

3. Write a paragraph about your city. (See page 95.)

4. Write a postcard to your friend, inviting him or her to visit you. (See page 86.)

5. Present your work to the class.

PRONUNCIATION

Listen and repeat. Notice how the first two words of each sentence join together.

I am reading. → I'm reading.

You are working. → You're working.

We are shopping. → We're shopping.

She is eating. → She's eating.

He is waiting. → He's waiting.

They are talking. → They're talking.

LEARNER LOG

Circle what you learned and write the page number where you learned it.

1. I can name different kinds of buildings.
   Yes   Maybe   No   Page _____

2. I can read a map.
   Yes   Maybe   No   Page _____

3. I can follow street directions.
   Yes   Maybe   No   Page _____

4. I can find information in a phone book.
   Yes   Maybe   No   Page _____

5. I can send a package or letter.
   Yes   Maybe   No   Page _____

6. I know when to use the present continuous or simple present tense.
   Yes   Maybe   No   Page _____

7. I can use prepositions of location.
   Yes   Maybe   No   Page _____

8. I can understand addresses and phone numbers.
   Yes   Maybe   No   Page _____

Did you answer *No*? Review the information with a partner.

Rank what you like to do best from 1 to 6. 1 is your favorite activity. Your teacher will help you.

☐ practice listening

☐ practice speaking

☐ practice reading

☐ practice writing

☐ learn grammar

☐ learn new vocabulary

In the next unit, I want to focus on

_____.

Health

- **Identify healthy and unhealthy activities**
- **Identify body parts**
- **Make an appointment by phone**
- **Use the simple past tense**
- **Identify and describe emergencies**
- **Read medicine labels**
- **Use the modal verb** *should*

LESSON 1 ## A healthy life

GOAL ▶ **Identify healthy and unhealthy activities**   *Life Skill*

 **Write the words under each picture.**

exercise	sleep	smoke	stress

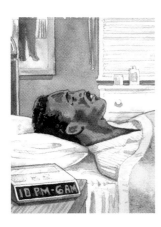   

_____ _____ _____ _____

 Which of these activities are healthy and which of them are unhealthy? Make sentences about each picture.

C **Read what doctors say about health and answer the questions *yes* or *no*.**

Most adults should sleep 6–8 hours a day.

1. Are you tired during the day? ____
2. Do you need more sleep? ____

Most adults should eat three balanced meals a day.

3. Do you eat three meals a day? ____
4. Do you take vitamins? ____

Most adults should exercise every day.

5. Do you exercise every day? ____
6. Do you have an exercise plan? ____

Most adults should see a doctor for a checkup regularly.

7. Do you go for a checkup every year? ____

Adults should not smoke.

8. Do you smoke? ____

D **Write three goals about your health.**

EXAMPLE: I need to stop drinking coffee.
I need to exercise more.

1. _____

2. _____

3. _____

  E **Active Task:** Find information about good health at your doctor's office or on the Internet. Bring it to class.

LESSON 2 What's the matter?

GOAL ▶ Identify body parts .... *Vocabulary*

 A **Look at the picture and write the words from the box next to each body part.**

shoulder(s)	arm(s)
eyes	head
neck	back
foot (feet)	leg(s)
nose	heart
chest	hand(s)
mouth	stomach

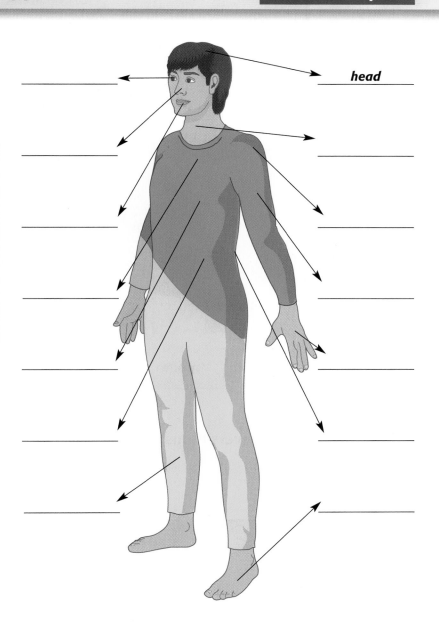

head

 B **Practice this conversation with the new words.**

Singular	Plural
Student A: What's the matter?	Student A: What's the matter?
Student B: My <u>head</u> hurt<u>s</u>.	Student B: My <u>shoulders</u> hurt.

C Look at the picture and write the words.

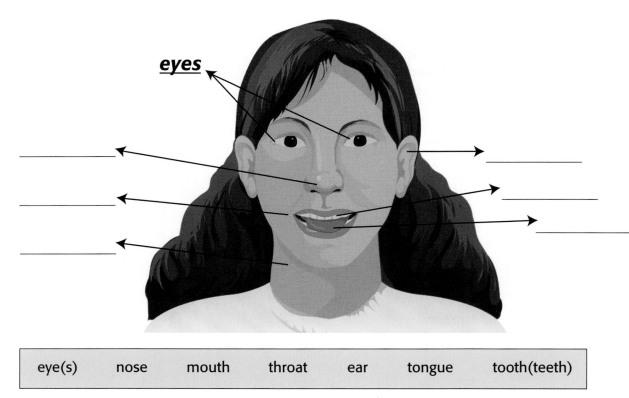

eyes

| eye(s) | nose | mouth | throat | ear | tongue | tooth(teeth) |

 D Listen to the conversations. Put the correct number under each picture.

_____ _____ _____ _____

E What other body parts do you need to know? Ask your teacher for help.

_____ _____ _____

_____ _____ _____

F **Write the correct word below each picture.**

| stomachache | toothache | headache | sore throat | backache |

Alexi

_____

Mario

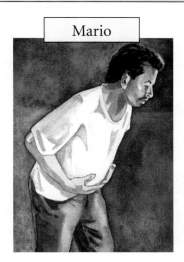

_____

Dalva

_____

Gilberto

_____

Marie

_____

 G **Practice this conversation with a partner. Use the words in exercise F.**

EXAMPLE:

Student A: What's the matter with Mario?

Student B: His stomach hurts. He has a stomachache.

Calling for an appointment

| GOAL ▶ Make an appointment by phone | Life Skill |

A Read the story. What's the matter with Alexi? Why is he nervous?

My name is Alexi. I'm from Russia. I like school and I want to learn English, but I don't come to school very much. I am tired a lot. I need to see a doctor, but I'm very nervous. My teacher says I need to go right now. He says the doctor can help me.

What is Alexi doing?
Who is he talking to?

  B First, draw a line from the questions to the answers. Then listen to the conversation.

What's your name?	1427 Hamilton St., New York City 12101.
What's your date of birth?	Yes.
Why do you want to see the doctor?	Alexi Tashkov.
What's your phone number?	Check. No, I don't.
Where do you live?	(212) 555-5755.
When can you see the doctor?	I'm tired all the time.
How will you pay? Do you have insurance?	Anytime Monday or Tuesday.
Are you a new patient?	June 28, 1961.

C Listen to these four conversations and fill in the information in the chart below.

	Name	Problem	Time	Pay method
	Alexi Tashkov	Tired	Anytime Mon. or Tue.	Check
1.				
2.				
3.				
4.				

D Now fill in this chart with your information. (Choose one of the illnesses from page 105. It doesn't have to be true!)

1. Name (What's your name?)	2. Problem (What's the matter?)	3. Time (When can you see the doctor?)	4. Pay method (How will you pay?)

E Use the information from your chart to make a conversation with your partner. Use the questions from the chart above.

Receptionist: Hello, Alliance Medical Offices. Can I help you?

Sick Student: Hello, I want to make an appointment to see Doctor Singh.

Receptionist: OK. What's your name?

Sick Student: _____

Receptionist: _____

Sick Student: _____

Receptionist: _____

Sick Student: _____

Receptionist: _____

Sick Student: _____

Receptionist: OK, please come in at _____ on _____.

Sick Student: Thank you, good-bye.

Going to the doctor

GOAL ▶ **Use the simple past tense**   *Grammar*

What is Alexi doing?
Does he look healthy?

A **Listen to Alexi and make sentences.**

Before Alexi got sick . . .

he walked	to a doctor every year.
he talked	soccer on weekends.
he played	a mile every day.
he smoked	a pack of cigarettes every day.

B **Listen to Alexi and make sentences.**

After Alexi got sick, . . .

he was	to smoke.
he went	to the doctor.
he continued	to stop smoking.
the doctor said	a heart attack.
he had	tired a lot.

C Listen again to Alexi. Then study the charts with your teacher.

Regular simple past = base + ed			
Base	Subject	Past	Example sentence
walk	I	walked	I <u>walked</u> a mile every day.
talk	he, she, it	talked	You <u>talked</u> to the doctor every year.
play	you, we	played	He <u>played</u> soccer on the weekends.
smoke	they	smoked	They <u>smoked</u> cigarettes every day.

Irregular simple past of the verb *be*			
Base	Subject	Past	Example sentence
be	I he, she, it	was	I <u>was</u> sick.
	you, we they	were	You <u>were</u> at the hospital.

Other irregular simple past verbs			
Base	Subject	Past	Example sentence
have	I, he, she,	had	I <u>had</u> a heart attack.
go	it, you,	went	We <u>went</u> to the doctor.
say	we, they	said	The doctor <u>said</u> to stop smoking.

D Ask a partner questions about Alexi before he was sick.

EXAMPLE:
Student A: What did Alexi do every day?
Student B: He smoked every day.

1. What did Alexi do every year? _____

2. What did he do every weekend? _____

3. What did he do every week? _____

E Ask a partner questions about Alexi after he got sick.

EXAMPLE:
Student A: Where did Alexi go?
Student B: He went to the doctor.

1. What did the doctor say? _____

2. What did Alexi continue to do? _____

3. What did Alexi have? _____

GOAL ▶ **Identify and describe emergencies**   *Vocabulary*

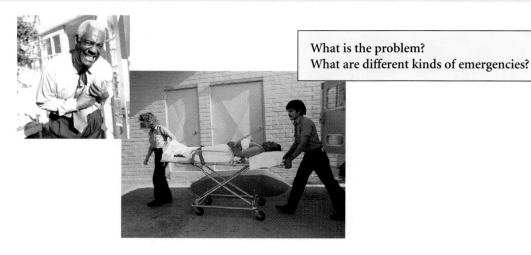

What is the problem?
What are different kinds of emergencies?

A **Listen and practice the conversation in pairs.**

Operator: 911. What is your emergency?
A Friend: It's a medical emergency.
Operator: What's the problem?
A Friend: My friend **has chest pains** .
Operator: I will send an ambulance immediately.
A Friend: Thank you.
Operator: What's your name and phone number, and where is your friend?
A Friend: My name is **Teresa, and my phone is 555-4334. I live at 9976 W. Burma St** .
My friend is here with me. Please hurry.

B **Practice the conversation with the words below. Use your address.**

is unconscious   is choking   has a broken nose   accidentally took poison

C Write the correct problem under each picture. Then go to exercises D and E below.

fever	headache	stomachache	cough

Problem _____

Medicine _____

Brand Name _____

Problem _____

Medicine _____

Brand Name _____

Problem _____

Medicine _____

Brand Name _____

Problem _____

Medicine _____

Brand Name _____

D What medicine do you need for each illness? Write the correct medicine under each illness above.

aspirin

cough syrup

antacid

E What's the *brand name* of the medicine you use? Write a medicine brand name with each picture in exercise C.

F **Complete the chart with a group.**

	Always call 911	Sometimes call 911	Never call 911	Take medicine	Brand name
She has a cold.			x	x	
A cat is in a tree.			x		
She has terrible chest pains.					
They have the flu.					
The man is not breathing.					
There is no food in the house.					
I am very tired.					
He coughs every day.					
She has a sore throat.					
She has a stomachache.					
She has a broken arm.					
He accidentally took poison.					

G **Make conversations about an illness or an emergency with a partner.**

EXAMPLE:
Student A: What's the matter?
Student B: I have chest pains.
Student A: You need to call a doctor right now.

H **Active Task:** Go to the drugstore and make a list of brand names for the different medicines in this lesson. Bring your list to class and compare it with other students.

 LESSON 6 Over-the-counter medicines

GOAL ▶ **Read medicine labels**   *Life Skill*

A **Find these words on the label and underline them.**

directions	aches and pains	symptoms	indications	exceed
tablets	warning	persist	teenagers	

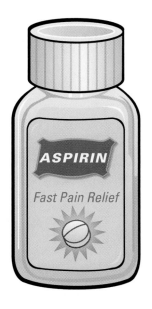

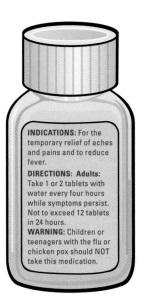

INDICATIONS: For the temporary relief of aches and pains and to reduce fever.
DIRECTIONS: Adults: Take 1 or 2 tablets with water every four hours while symptoms persist. Not to exceed 12 tablets in 24 hours.
WARNING: Children or teenagers with the flu or chicken pox should NOT take this medication.

ASPIRIN

Fast Pain Relief

B **Draw lines to match the words on the left with the examples on the right.**

Directions	for headache
Indications	don't drive
Warning	take two tablets

C **Match the words on the left with the corresponding words on the right.**

teenager	aches, pains, and fever
symptoms	continues
not to exceed	13–18 years old
persists	no more than

D Match each direction, indication, and warning to the correct medicine. Write the correct letter in the spaces below.

_____ **Warning:** Children or teenagers with the flu or chicken pox should NOT take this medication.

_____ **Warning:** Do not take more than 10 tablets in 24 hours.

_____ **Warning:** If sore throat pain persists or coughing is acute, contact your doctor.

_____ **Directions:** Chew 2–4 tablets as needed.

_____ **Directions:** Adults: Take 1 or 2 tablets with water every four hours while symptoms persist. Not to exceed 12 tablets in 24 hours.

_____ **Directions:** Take two teaspoons every four hours for pain.

_____ **Indications:** For temporary relief of headache or muscle aches and fever.

_____ **Indications:** For temporary relief of cough and throat irritation due to infections.

_____ **Indications:** For fast relief of acid indigestion and stomach pain.

a.

Cough Syrup

b.

Aspirin

c.

Antacid

E Read the labels in exercise D and answer the questions. Fill in the circle next to the correct answer.

1. How often can you take aspirin?
   ○ once a day   ○ 1 to 2 tablets every day   ○ 1 to 2 tablets every four hours

2. What type of medicine is the antacid?
   ○ syrup   ○ chewable tablet   ○ capsule

3. Cough syrup is for coughs and . . .
   ○ throat irritation   ○ headache   ○ stomachache

F **Active Task:** Find a medicine label at home or look up a brand name medication on the Internet. Discuss the directions with your class.

7 The doctor's advice

GOAL ▶ **Use the modal verb *should***   *Grammar*

A Look at the label. Then read the sentences below.
What should Gilberto do?
Write *yes* or *no*.

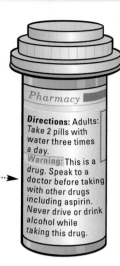

> **Directions:** Adults: Take two pills with water three times a day.
>
> **Warning:** This is a drug. Speak to a doctor before taking with other drugs including aspirin. Never drive or drink alcohol while taking this drug.

___no___ Gilberto should take the medicine and drive.

____ Gilberto should take two pills three times a day.

____ Gilberto should take the pills with water.

____ Gilberto should take three pills two times a day.

____ Gilberto should drink alcohol with the medicine.

____ Gilberto should take aspirin with the medicine.

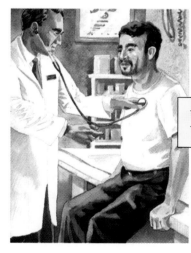

> Where is Gilberto?
> What is the doctor saying?

B Listen to Gilberto's doctor and mark with a ✔ what Gilberto *should* do.

- ✔ Exercise every day
- ☐ Walk every day
- ☐ Sleep 10 hours every night
- ☐ Eat fatty foods
- ☐ Smoke
- ☐ Run every two days
- ☐ Take his medicine

C Study the chart with your teacher.

Modal verb *should* (Affirmative)			
Subject	**Modal verb**	**Base**	
I, you, he,	should	take	two pills three times a day.
she, it		exercise	every day.
we, they		sleep	eight hours a day.
		eat	three meals a day.

Gilberto should take two pills three times a day.

Modal verb *should* (Negative)				
Subject	**Modal verb**	**Not**	**Base**	
I, you, he	should	not	drink	alcohol with the medicine.
she, it	(shouldn't)		take	aspirin with the medicine.
we, they			eat	fatty foods with the medicine.
			drive	and take the medicine.

Gilberto <u>should not</u> drink alcohol with the medicine.
Gilberto <u>shouldn't</u> drink alcohol with the medicine.

D **Make sentences about what Gilberto should and shouldn't do.**

1. Exercise every day. → Gilberto should exercise every day.

2. Smoke. → Gilberto shouldn't smoke.

3. Walk every day. _____

4. Run every two days. _____

5. Sleep 10 hours every night. _____

6. Eat fatty foods. _____

E **Ask a partner what Gilberto should and shouldn't do. Use these words:**
exercise, smoke, drink alcohol, sleep, take medicine, and eat fatty foods.

EXAMPLE: What should Gilberto do?
          He should <u>**exercise**</u> every day.

F **What goals do you have for your health? What should you do?**

I should . . . _____

_____

I shouldn't . . . _____

_____

Review

A Label the picture with the vocabulary you know.

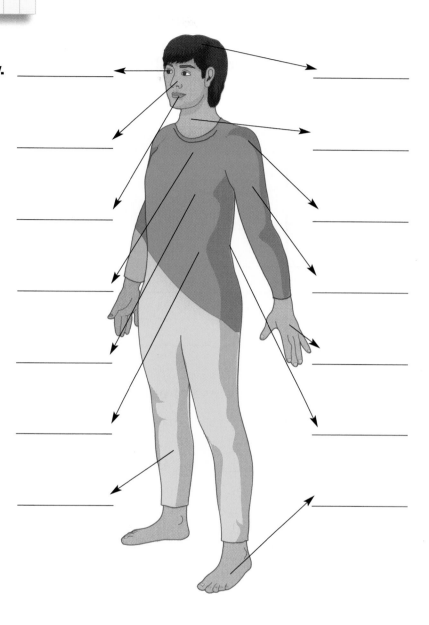

_____

_____

_____

_____

_____

_____

_____

_____

_____

_____

_____

_____

B Draw a line from the illness to the advice.

1. I have a headache.

2. I have a bad toothache.

3. I have a stomachache.

4. I have chest pains.

a. You should go to a dentist.

b. You should call 911 right now.

c. You should take some aspirin.

d. You should take some antacid tablets.

C Give someone advice on how to stay healthy. Write two things they should do and two things they shouldn't do.

1.   2.   3.   4.

1. _____

2. _____

3. _____

4. _____

D Write the past tense of each verb.

1. Yesterday I _____ (have) a terrible stomachache.

2. Suzanne _____ (be) late for work this morning.

3. Last summer we _____ (play) soccer every weekend.

4. I _____ (go) to the doctor on Monday.

5. I _____ (take) some aspirin this morning.

6. Last year I _____ (break) my arm.

7. The doctor _____ (say) I shouldn't smoke.

8. They _____ (be) on vacation last week.

E Make a list of words and phrases you learned in this unit for talking about illnesses and emergencies. Which ones are most useful?

1. *make an appointment* _____

2. _____

3. _____

4. _____

5. _____

6. _____

7. _____

8. _____

9. _____

10. _____

T E A M P R O J E C T

Making a health pamphlet

1. Form a team with four or five students. Your group is a committee who will design a public service pamphlet for parents. The pamphlet will give parents some health tips and tell them what medicine they should take for common illnesses.

   In your team you need:

Position	Job	Student Name
Student 1 Team Leader	See that everyone speaks English. See that everyone participates.	
Student 2	Give advice on medicine for three illnesses.	
Student 3	Give advice on three things to do to stay healthy.	
Student 4	Prepare a class presentation with help from the team.	

2. Write three things people should do to be healthy, and three things they should not do. (See pages 101–102.)

3. What are three illnesses to include in your pamphlet? (See pages 103–105.)

4. What medications should people take for these illnesses? (See pages 111–112.)

5. Design a pamphlet with pictures to present the information.

6. Prepare a presentation for the class.

PRONUNCIATION

We pronounce the *ed* past tense ending in different ways. Listen to the tape. Underline the /d/ sounds. Draw a circle around the /t/ sounds. Draw a square around the /id/ sounds.

Listen and repeat.

played   smoked   decided   walked   stayed   hated
liked   answered   invited   asked   called   wanted

LEARNER LOG

Circle what you learned and write the page number where you learned it.

1. I can make health goals.
   Yes   Maybe   No   Page _____

2. I can identify body parts.
   Yes   Maybe   No   Page _____

3. I can talk about aches and pains.
   Yes   Maybe   No   Page _____

4. I can use the telephone.
   Yes   Maybe   No   Page _____

5. I can make a doctor's appointment.
   Yes   Maybe   No   Page _____

6. I can read labels on medicine.
   Yes   Maybe   No   Page _____

7. I can use the simple past.
   Yes   Maybe   No   Page _____

8. I can use the modal verb *should.*
   Yes   Maybe   No   Page _____

Did you answer *No?* Review the information with a partner.

Rank what you like to do best from 1 to 6. 1 is your favorite activity. Your teacher will help you.

[ ] practice listening

[ ] practice speaking

[ ] practice reading

[ ] practice writing

[ ] learn grammar

[ ] learn new words (vocabulary)

In the next unit, I want to focus on

_____

UNIT 7

Work, Work, Work

GOALS
- Evaluate learning and work skills
- Identify jobs
- Read classified ads
- Fill out a job application
- Use the simple past in the negative
- Use *can* to describe ability
- Follow instructions

LESSON 1 What is a good student?

GOAL ▶ Evaluate learning and work skills | *Life Skill*

A **Are you a good student? Answer *Yes* or *No*.**

Yes No
- ☐ ☐ I come to class every day.
- ☐ ☐ I come to class on time.
- ☐ ☐ I participate in class.
- ☐ ☐ I participate in groups.

Yes No
- ☐ ☐ I take notes in class.
- ☐ ☐ I always do my homework.
- ☐ ☐ I listen carefully.
- ☐ ☐ I help others.

B **What are two things you can do well (at school or at work)?**

EXAMPLE: *I can fix cars.*

I can _____

I can _____

C **What are two things you can't do (at school or at work), but want to learn?**

EXAMPLE: *I can't use a computer* _____, but I want to learn.

I can't _____, but I want to learn.

I can't _____, but I want to learn.

D **Read about Dalva.**

My name is Dalva and I'm a student at Casper Education Center. I'm learning English. Sometimes it's difficult. I also have a part-time job in an office. At work and at school it's very important to work with people in teams.

E **Read Dalva's work evaluation form. What can Dalva do well?**

EXAMPLE: Dalva can ***follow instructions*** _____.

1. Dalva can _____.

2. Dalva can _____.

EMPLOYEE EVALUATION FORM
Fairview Hotel

Employee Name: **Dalva Mendes**
Position: **Administrative Assistant**
Date: **March 4**

EVALUATION:

Comes to work on time.   S   Ⓖ   NI

Follows instructions.   Ⓢ   G   NI

Helps others.   Ⓢ   G   NI

Works well with the team.   Ⓢ   G   NI

Understands the job.   S   G   ⓃⒾ
New employee. She is still learning.

Has a positive attitude.   Ⓢ   G   NI
Enjoys her job and is always cheerful.

Supervisor's signature: *Patricia Macias*
Employee's signature: *Dalva Mendes*

S = Superior   G = Good   NI = Needs improvement

F **In groups, talk about which skills are most important in the evaluation and why. Number the skills from 1 to 6. (1 is most important.)**

____ Comes to work on time.

____ Follows instructions.

____ Helps others.

____ Works well with the team.

____ Understands the job.

____ Has a positive attitude.

GOAL ▶ Identify jobs

A Write the job titles under the correct pictures.

| cashier | delivery person | gardener | police officer |
| custodian | doctor | mechanic | homemaker |

Kristina

_____

Esteban

_____

Ivan

_____

Maria

_____

Amy

_____

Chang

_____

Geraldo

_____

Phuong

_____

B Take turns asking about each job.

EXAMPLE: **Student A:** What does Geraldo do?
Student B: He's a police officer.

C Write the jobs from page 123 in the correct circles. Add any other job titles that you know.

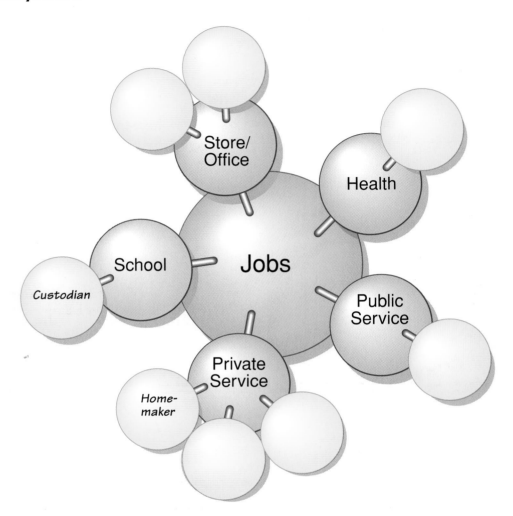

D Which jobs from page 123 do you like best?

Jobs I like:

1. _____

2. _____

3. _____

4. _____

Jobs I don't like:

1. _____

2. _____

3. _____

4. _____

E **Practice the conversation with a partner.**

Student A: Excuse me. Do you work?

Student B: Yes, I do.
Student A: What do you do?
Student B: I'm a cook.
Student A: Do you like it?
Student B: Yes, I do. / No, not really.

Student B: No, I don't. I'm a student.
Student A: Do you like it?
Student B: Yes, I do. / No, not really.

F **Practice the conversation with five students in the class and write the information.**

Name	What does he or she do?

G **Make a bar graph of the jobs in your group.**

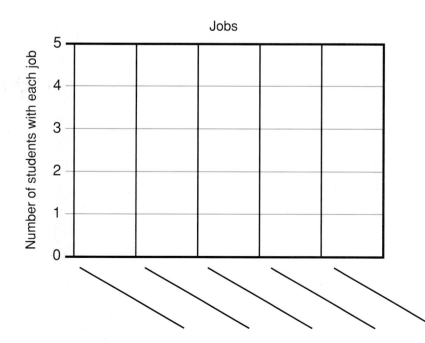

LESSON 3 Help wanted

GOAL ▶ Read classified ads   *Life Skill*

A Look at the classified ads. Write the correct jobs in the chart below the ads.

Daily News Classified Ads

Employment

Apartment Manager,
2 yrs exp, free rent, speak Spanish and English, full-time, paint and minor maintenance. Available immediately.

Call Manor Apartments 555-8976

CASHIER
P/T, $6/hr., Franklin's Cinema, n/exp. OK, Call for appl. 555-3344

★★★★★★★★★★★
FULL-TIME COOK!

No experience needed, training available, Martha's Kitchen, good hours, apply in person,

3456 W. Melrose, Hill City, 8am–5pm

DRIVER
Alexander's Furniture Warehouse

Make deliveries to homes in Hill City, drivers licence, driving experience necessary, FT, $10/hr Monday–Friday, 6am–2:30pm
Call Alexander 555-3300

LEGAL ASSISTANT
45 wpm, filing, F/T great opportunity, Smith and Peterson Law office, speak English,

Call 555-9988

ESL TEACHER
Casper Education ★ Center ★

BA required, 1 yr teaching exp, PT positions only, resume req., benefits, Call Nancy 555-2000

Information	Jobs
Full-time	
Part-time	
Paid hourly	
Needs a BA degree	
Needs a driver's license	
Needs experience	

B What do these abbreviations mean?

p/t _____   exp. _____

FT _____   yrs _____

wpm _____   req. _____

BA _____   appl. _____

C Listen to these people talking about the classified job ads on page 126. Write the titles of the jobs they're talking about.

1. _____

2. _____

3. _____

4. _____

D Read the paragraphs below and decide which job from page 126 is good for each person.

1. Silvia is a hard worker. She can work full-time or part-time. She speaks English well. She can work in an office and knows how to type. Which job is good for Silvia?

   _____

2. Tanh is always on time for work. He has a driver's license and knows how to drive a truck. Which job is good for Tanh?

   _____

3. Lucrecia has three children and wants to stay home with them. She needs to work. She can fix things around the house and is very organized. Her rent is very expensive. Which job is good for Lucrecia?

   _____

4. Robert needs a full time position. He doesn't have any experience. He wants to learn something new. Which job is good for Robert?

   _____

E Which job in exercise A do you like best? Which job do you dislike?

F **Active Task:** Find jobs in a local newspaper or on the Internet. Find two jobs you can do and tell the class.

LESSON 4 Applying for a job

GOAL ▶ Fill out a job application

Life Skill

 Read Dalva's job application.

APPLICATION FOR EMPLOYMENT AT THE PACIFIC HOTEL

PERSONAL INFORMATION

Name   Last   First   MI
         Mendes   *Dalva*   *M.*

Date   *12/10/02*

Address   *2376 Monroe Street, San Diego, CA 92101*

Social Security Number   *5X7-X7-XX00*

Phone   *(619) 555-6849*

Position applied for   *Front desk clerk*

SKILLS

Typing: *65 wpm.*   Computer skills: *Internet and word processing*

Languages: *Spanish, French, Portuguese, and English (written and spoken)*

JOB HISTORY (List most recent positions first)

Job title: *Administrative assistant at Fairview Hotel*
Dates: *December 2001–November 30, 2002*
Reason for leaving: *Want to use languages more*

Job title: *Cashier at La Tostada restaurant*
Dates: *June 1998–November 2001*
Reason for leaving: *Moved*

WORK AVAILABILITY: *Daytime or evenings*

EDUCATION

    Casper Education Center 1998–2000: Computer and English language studies

REFERENCES

1. *Patricia Macias   Office Manager   Fairview Hotel   (515) 555-5454*
2. *Delia Johnson   Owner   La Tostada restaurant   (714) 555-5734*

B **What are the six sections of the job application?**

1. _____

2. _____

3. _____

4. _____

5. _____

6. _____

C **Answer the questions about Dalva's job application.**

1. What job is she applying for?

_____

2. What languages can she speak?

_____

3. What skills does she have?

_____

4. When is she available to work?

_____

5. Who are her references?

_____

D **Write two more questions about Dalva's application. Ask your partner.**

1. _____

2. _____

E Fill out the application with your information.

APPLICATION FOR EMPLOYMENT AT THE PACIFIC HOTEL

PERSONAL INFORMATION

Name   Last   First   MI

_____

Date _____

Address _____

Social Security Number *XXX-XX-XXXX* _____

Phone _____

Position applied for _____

SKILLS

Typing: _____   **Computer skills:** _____

Languages: _____

JOB HISTORY (List most recent positions first)

Job title: _____

Dates: _____

Reason for leaving: _____

 F Practice asking for an application.

1. Excuse me. I'm interested in a job. Do you have an application?
2. May I have an application, please?
3. Do you have any openings? Could I have an application, please?

  Active Task: Go to a local business or restaurant or look at their web site. Ask for or print out a work application. Bring the application to class.

5 A job interview

GOAL ▶ Use the simple past in the negative   *Grammar*

JOB HISTORY (List most recent positions first)

Job title: *Administrative assistant at Fairview Hotel*

Dates: *December 2001–November 30, 2002*

Reason for leaving: *Want to use languages more*

Job title: *Cashier at La Tostada restaurant*

Dates: *June 1998–November 2001*

Reason for leaving: *Moved*

What is Dalva doing?
Who is she talking to?

A **Listen to the conversation and read it with a partner.**

Mrs. Cardoza: Good afternoon, Ms. Mendes. Please sit down. I have your application here. You were a desk clerk at the Fairview Hotel and before that you were a cashier, is that right?

Dalva: I was an administrative assistant at the Fairview Hotel. I wasn't a desk clerk.

Mrs. Cardoza: Oh yes, that's right. What kind of work did you do?

Dalva: I checked reservations and typed letters.

Mrs. Cardoza: So you didn't answer the phone or talk to guests?

Dalva: No, I didn't talk to the guests, but I learn quickly and I speak many languages.

Mrs. Cardoza: Did you work in the evenings?

Dalva: No, I didn't work in the evenings. I finished at 6:30 P.M.

Mrs. Cardoza: Thank you, Ms. Mendes. We'll call you.

B **Are these sentences true or false? On a separate piece of paper, rewrite the false statements using the negative.**

<u>True</u> 1. Dalva was a cashier at La Tostada restaurant.

_____ 2. Dalva was a desk clerk at the Fairview Hotel.

_____ 3. Dalva answered the phone at the Fairview Hotel.

_____ 4. Dalva talked to guests at the Fairview Hotel.

C **Study the charts with your teacher.**

Regular simple past = base + *ed*			
Base	**Subject**	**Past**	**Example sentence**
check	I, he, she,	checked	Dalva **checked** reservations.
work	it, we	worked	I **worked** as a driver.
cook	you, they	cooked	They **cooked** lunch and dinner.

Regular negative simple past = *did + not* (*didn't*) + base			
Subject	**did + not**	**Base**	**Example sentence**
I, he, she,	didn't	answer	Dalva **didn't answer** the phone.
it, we		work	We **didn't work** in the evenings.
you, they			

Simple past of the verb *be*			
Base	**Subject**	**Past**	**Example sentence**
be	I, he, she, it	was	Dalva **was** a cashier.
	we, you, they	were	You **were** at a hotel.

Negative simple past of *be* = *was + not* (*wasn't*) or *were + not* (*weren't*)			
Subject	**Past**	**not**	**Example sentence**
I, he, she, it	was	not	Dalva **wasn't** a desk clerk.
we, you, they	were		You **weren't** at a restaurant.

D **Change the statements to the negative.**

EXAMPLE: Dalva was a student in 1997.
          Dalva **wasn't** a student in 1997. She was a student in 1999.

1. Dalva moved in 1999.

   Dalva _____ in 1999. She moved in 2001.

2. Dalva worked at the Fairmont Hotel.

   Dalva _____ at the Fairmont Hotel. She worked at the Fairview Hotel.

3. Dalva and Mrs. Cardoza talked about food.

   Dalva and Mrs. Cardoza _____ about food. They talked about Dalva's work

   experience.

4. Dalva and Mrs. Cardoza were angry.

   Dalva and Mrs. Cardoza _____ angry. They were friendly.

A second interview

GOAL ▶ Use *can* to describe ability   *Grammar*

SKILLS

Typing: *65 wpm.*   Computer skills: *Internet and word processing*

Languages: *Spanish, French, Portuguese, and English (written and spoken)*

A **Listen and practice the conversation with a partner.**

Mrs. Cardoza: Dalva, can you use a computer?
Dalva: Yes, I can type and I use e-mail all the time.
Mrs. Cardoza: That's great. Can you type in English?
Dalva: Yes, I can type 65 words per minute. I learned in school.
Mrs. Cardoza: We need an assistant to answer e-mails and confirm reservations.
Dalva: Really? I can do that.
Mrs. Cardoza: Great! When can you start?
Dalva: I can start today!

B **Look at the conversation again and at Dalva's job application form on page 128. What can Dalva do?**

1. Type: *Dalva can type 65 words per minute.* _____

2. Use: _____

3. Speak: _____

4. Start: _____

C Learn how to use the verb *can.* Study the charts with your teacher.

Simple present = subject + *can* + base			
Subject	**can**	**Base**	**Sentence**
I, you, he, she, it, we, they	can	type	Dalva can type.

Negative = subject + *can* + *not* (= *can't*) + base			
Subject	**can't**	**Base**	**Sentence**
I, you, he, she, it, we, they	can't	cook	I can't cook.

Question = *can* + subject + base			
can	**Subject**	**Base**	**Sentence**
Can	I, you, he, she, it, we, they	speak	Can he speak Spanish?

D Make a list of six things you can do.

1. _____
2. _____
3. _____
4. _____
5. _____
6. _____

E Use your list to ask your partner six questions.

EXAMPLE:
Student A: Can you swim?
Student B: Yes, I can. / No, I can't.

F Make sentences about you and your partner.

EXAMPLE:
We can swim.
Roberto can type, but I can't.

How does it work?

GOAL ▶ **Follow instructions**

A **Write the correct letter next to each machine in the picture.**

a. copier   c. computer   e. printer

b. fax   d. shredder   f. answering machine

Where is Dalva?
What is she doing?

B **Write the instructions for the copier. Put the instructions in the correct order.**

_____ Choose the number of copies.

_____ Place the original on the glass.

_ *1* _ Turn on the unit.

_____ Press the start button.

_____ Close the lid.

C **Use the words in the box to complete the sentences below. You may use some words more than once. Then write the correct number next to each picture.**

Connect	Press	Turn on	Turn off
Keep	Enter	Record	Place

1. _____ the machine.

   _____ the paper carefully in the slot.

   _____ fingers away from the machine.

   _____ the machine after the paper is destroyed.

   ____

2. _____ the paper in the machine.

   _____ the number.

   _____ start.

   ____

3. _____ the machine to the phone.

   _____ the button that says *Message*.

   _____ your message onto the tape.

   ____

D **Choose a machine that you use at home or at work.**
For example: microwave, oven, washing machine. Give instructions for how to use this machine, but don't say the name of the machine. The other students will guess!

Review

EMPLOYMENT HISTORY

Company: **Datamix Computers**
Position: **Computer programmer**
Dates: **June 1999–present**

Company: **Datamix Computers**
Position: **Assembly worker**
Dates: **May 1997–June 1999**

Youssouf Fosso

 A **Read the information about Youssouf and complete the sentences below with the correct negative or positive form of the verb.**

EXAMPLE: Youssouf ____*didn't work*____ (work) at Datamix Computers in 1996.

1. Youssouf _____ (be) an assembly worker at Datamix Computers in 1998.

2. Youssouf _____ (start) his job at Datamix in May 1997.

3. Youssouf _____ (be) a programmer from May 1997 to June 1998.

4. Youssouf _____ (change) his job in May 1999.

SKILLS

Languages: **French–bilingual (fluent in reading, writing, listening, and speaking)**
Typing skills: **35 wpm**
Computer skills: **Advanced programming, knowledge of many software programs**

 B **Write sentences about what Youssouf can and can't do.**

1. speak French **Youssouf can speak French.** _____

2. speak Spanish _____

3. type 50 wpm _____

4. use the computer _____

Review

C **Write the name of the job under the picture.**

1. m _ _ _ _ _ _ c

3. c _ _ _ _ _ _ _ n

5. d _ _ _ _ _ _ y
person

2. g _ _ _ _ _ r

4. c _ _ _ _ _ r

6. h _ _ _ _ _ _ r

D **Look at the picture and identify the machine.** _____

E **Match the correct verb with the instruction.**

1. _____ the paper in the machine.   a. Press
2. _____ the number.   b. Place
3. _____ start.   c. Enter

T E A M P R O J E C T

Making your own company

1. Form teams with four or five students. You are going to make a new company, make job advertisements and interview new employees.

   In your team, you need:

Position	Job	Student Name
Student 1 Team Leader	See that everyone speaks English. See that everyone participates.	
Student 2	Write a classified ad with help from the team.	
Student 3	Prepare an application form.	
Student 4	Prepare interview questions.	

2. You are the owners of a new company. What is the name of your company? What kind of company is it?

3. What job are you going to advertise? What information will you put in the advertisement? (See page 126.)

4. What questions can you have on the application form? What questions can you ask at the job interview? (See pages 128, 131, and 133.)

5. Interview four students.

6. Decide on who you will hire and present your work to the class.

PRONUNCIATION

Which words are stressed in these questions? Listen and repeat. Look at the example. Mark the stressed words in each question.

● · · ●

Where do you **work?**   Where does he work?

What do you **do?**   What does he do?

When can you **start?**   When can he start?

LEARNER LOG

Circle what you learned and write the page number where you learned it.

1. I can describe jobs.
   Yes   Maybe   No   Page _____

2. I can read classified ads for jobs.
   Yes   Maybe   No   Page _____

3. I can read a job application.
   Yes   Maybe   No   Page _____

4. I can fill out a job application.
   Yes   Maybe   No   Page _____

5. I can describe my abilities and skills.
   Yes   Maybe   No   Page _____

6. I can use the simple past in the negative.
   Yes   Maybe   No   Page _____

7. I can use *can* and *can't.*
   Yes   Maybe   No   Page _____

Did you answer *No?* Review the information with a partner.

Rank what you like to do best from 1 to 6. 1 is your favorite activity. Your teacher will help you.

☐ practice listening

☐ practice speaking

☐ practice reading

☐ practice writing

☐ learn grammar

☐ learn new words (vocabulary)

In the next unit, I want to focus on

_____.

UNIT 8

Goals and Lifelong Learning

GOALS

- Set your own goals
- Describe academic goals
- Use infinitive verb forms
- Use *going to*
- Write a paragraph about goals
- Ask for and find help
- Learn about places to learn

LESSON 1   What are your goals?

GOAL ▶ Set your own goals   *Life Skill*

Where is Lien?
What is she doing?

 A **Listen to Lien's story and check what Lien wants to do.**

___ She wants to buy a house.

___ She wants to get a better job.

___ She wants to get a job.

___ She wants to get married.

___ She wants to graduate from a university.

___ She wants to have children.

___ She wants to keep a job.

✔ She wants to speak English better.

___ She wants to go to a university.

___ She wants to become a U.S. citizen.

___ She wants to go to college.

___ She wants to participate in her child's school.

___ She wants to return to her first country.

___ She wants to move.

B **Look at Lien's goals on page 141. Put them in the correct box.**

Personal and Family

Education
She wants to speak English better.

Career (Work)

C **Write two sentences in each section about what you want to do.**

Personal and Family:

1. _____

2. _____

Education:

1. *I want to speak English.* _____

2. _____

Career:

1. _____

2. _____

| GOAL ▶ Describe academic goals | *Vocabulary* |

A Find out about the educational system in your area. Fill in the missing information in the chart below. Your teacher will help you.

Elementary School	Middle/Junior High School	High School	Adult
Approximate ages of students: _____	Approximate ages of students: _____	Approximate ages of students: _____	Adult schools Junior colleges / Community colleges
Years to complete: _____	Years to complete: _____	Years to complete: _____	Colleges/Universities Trade schools

B Ask your partner questions about the pie chart.

EXAMPLE:

Student A: What percentage of people in the United States have less than a high school diploma?

Student B: Seventeen point one per cent.

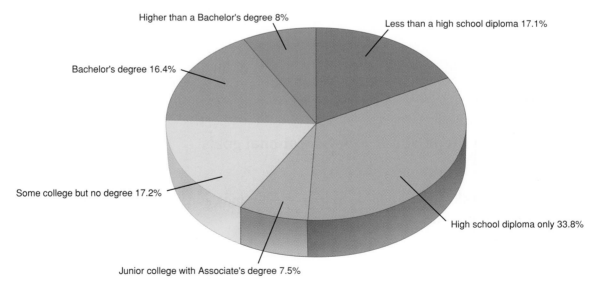

Higher than a Bachelor's degree 8%

Less than a high school diploma 17.1%

Bachelor's degree 16.4%

Some college but no degree 17.2%

High school diploma only 33.8%

Junior college with Associate's degree 7.5%

*Figures from US Department of Commerce, Bureau of the Census

C Compare education in the United States to the educational system in your first country.

D Read the descriptions of different schools.

Adult schools	These schools are sometimes free. Students learn basic skills like reading and writing. They can learn about jobs and computers. These schools can help students get their GED.
Junior colleges/ Community colleges	These schools are not expensive for residents. They offer two-year academic, technical, and vocational courses. They help students prepare for universities or a job. Students can study part-time, in the evenings or on weekends.
Colleges/Universities	These schools prepare students for jobs and careers. They are often very expensive. They offer four-year academic courses.
Trade schools	These schools are sometimes expensive. They help students learn job-related skills such as computers or mechanics.

E Match the question with the answers by writing the correct letter next to each question.

_**b**_ Why is it good to get a high school diploma?

____ Why do people go to a two-year college?

____ Why do people go to a university?

____ Why do people go to an adult school?

a. To learn to read and write English.
   To get a GED.

b. To get a better job.
   To prepare to go to a two-year college or a university.

c. To get an Associate's degree.
   To prepare for a better job.
   To prepare to go to a university.

d. To qualify for a career.
   To get a Bachelor's degree.

F Talk to a friend about your educational goals.

 G **Active Task:** Go to a college in your town or look at its web site and find a course description guide. Bring it to school to discuss.

BA/BS or Bachelor's degree—a Bachelor of Arts or a Bachelor of Science degree from a college or university, usually after four years of study

AA/AS or Associate's degree—an Associate of Arts or an Associate of Science degree from a junior college after two years of study

GED—General Equivalency Diploma (equivalent to high school diploma)

GOAL ▶ Use infinitive verb forms

Grammar

A **Close your book and listen to Lien's story. Then read about Lien's work goals.**

Lien has many goals. She wants to have a career. She wants to be a counselor in an adult school or a college because she wants to help people. She needs to go to school for many years to study but first she needs to learn English. She plans to go to Clear Mountain Adult School for two more years. There she is going to learn English and get her GED. Lien also needs to work. She needs a part-time job now and later she wants to work at a school for more experience.

What is Lien holding? Why is she happy?

Lien's plan

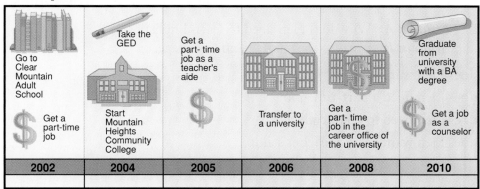

Go to Clear Mountain Adult School / Get a part-time job	Take the GED / Start Mountain Heights Community College	Get a part-time job as a teacher's aide	Transfer to a university	Get a part-time job in the career office of the university	Graduate from university with a BA degree / Get a job as a counselor
2002	2004	2005	2006	2008	2010

B **Study the chart and then talk about Lien's plans with another student.**

EXAMPLE:
Student A: What does Lien want to do in 2004?
Student B: She plans to get her GED.

Study the chart with your teacher.

When a verb follows *want, plan,* or *need,* use *to* before it.

Subject	Verb	Infinitive (*to + base*)	
I, you, we, they	want, need, plan	to	study
			graduate
he, she, it	wants, needs, plans		get

EXAMPLES:
I want to graduate in spring.   She needs to get a part-time job.
We plan to move to Florida.   He plans to study computers.
They need to study English.

  Listen to Lien's story again. Write what she needs and wants to do.

Wants	Needs
She wants to have a career.	

E **You can use *because* to answer the question *why.* Ask a partner questions.**

EXAMPLE: **Student A:** Why does Lien need to learn English?
         Student B: Because she wants to go to college.

1. Why does Lien want to be a counselor?
2. Why does Lien need a part-time job?
3. Why does Lien need to go to college?
4. Why does Lien want to be a teacher's aide?

What is Mario's job now?
What does he plan to do?
What do you think of his plan?

F **Read Mario's plans.**

Mario's plan

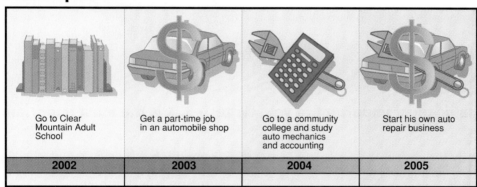

Go to Clear Mountain Adult School	Get a part-time job in an automobile shop	Go to a community college and study auto mechanics and accounting	Start his own auto repair business
2002	2003	2004	2005

G **Complete the sentences.**

1. Mario needs to go to Clear Mountain Adult School because he wants to learn English.

2. Mario wants to _____ because he wants experience in auto repair.

3. Mario plans to _____ because he wants to study auto mechanics and accounting.

4. Mario needs to _____ because he wants to be self-employed.

H **What are your plans? Write one sentence.**

I need to _____ *because I want to* _____ .

_____

GOAL ▶ Use *going to*

What is success?
Some people think that success is a
   good job and a lot of money.
Others say it is love and family.
What is success to you?

A **Rank what is most important to you. Write 1–5. 1 is the most important to you.**

_____ family   _____ a good job

_____ friends   _____ fun and entertainment

_____ money   _____ education

B **Read about what is important to Marie.**

   My career is most important to me. I am going to study nursing and work part-time as a home health aide. Then I am going to get my degree in nursing and become a registered nurse. I am going to work in a hospital. I am going to try to save money because I want to get married soon. My boyfriend's name is Jean. After we get married, we are going to have children, I hope. Maybe there will be some money to go to the movies sometimes, too. I'm going to work hard to make my plans come true.

C **With a group, rank what you think is important to Marie. Then share your ideas with another group.**

_____ family   _____ a good job

_____ friends   _____ fun and entertainment

_____ money   _____ education

Learn to talk about the future with *going to*. Study the chart with your teacher.

Subject	Future	Base	Example Sentences
I	am going to	be a nurse.	I am going to be a nurse.
You, we, they	are going to	work hard.	They are going to work hard.
He, she, it	is going to	save money.	She is going to save money.

Lien only:

- Get a GED
- Go to a university
- Become a tutor
- Become a counselor

Both Lien and Marie:

- Work part-time
- Study English at Clear Mountain Adult School
- Go to college
- Get a college degree

Marie only:

- Become a registered nurse
- Work in a hospital

E **Write sentences in the future about Lien and Marie's plans.**

1. *Lien is going to be a counselor.* _____

2. *Marie is going to study nursing.* _____

3. _____

4. _____

5. _____

6. _____

7. _____

8. _____

9. _____

10. _____

F Look at these goals. Check (✔) the goals you have.

— To go to college.

— To buy a house.

— To get a better job.

— To get a job.

— To get married.

— To graduate from a junior college with an Associate's degree.

— To go to a university.

— To graduate from a university.

— To have children.

— To keep a job.

✔ To speak English.

— To become a U.S. citizen.

— To participate in your child's school.

— To return to your country.

— To buy a car.

— To move.

— To travel around the world.

G Write your goal, your partner's goal, and one goal you both have.

You	Your partner
I am going to _____	My partner is going to _____
_____	_____
_____	_____

You and your partner

We are going to _____

_____

_____

H Tell a group about your plans for the future.

5 My goals

GOAL ▶ Write a paragraph about goals   *Academic Skill*

A Look at the pictures. What is happening in each picture?

_____

_____

_____

_____

_____

_____

_____

_____

B Write the sentences under the correct picture.

Marie plans to have children.   Marie plans to get married.

Marie plans to work in a hospital.   Marie plans to get a degree in nursing.

C Write the sentences in order. Use *first, second, third,* and *fourth.* See page 148 for help.

First, Marie plans to get a degree in nursing. _____

Second, _____

Third, _____

Fourth, _____

D **Study the paragraph with your teacher.**

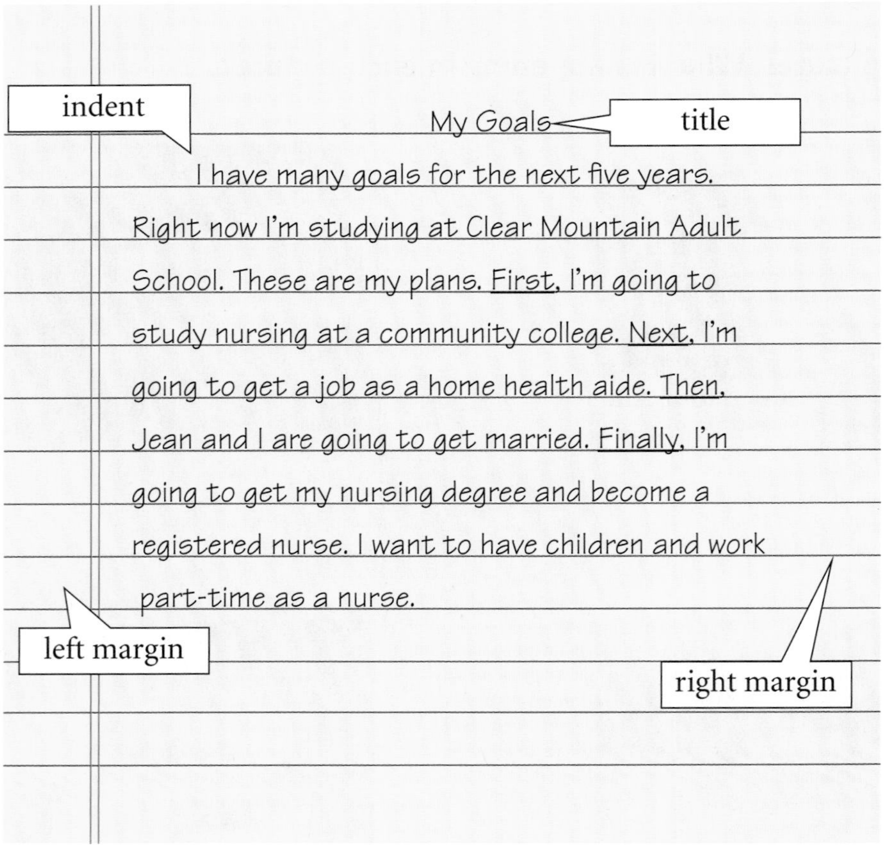

indent

My Goals ← title

  I have many goals for the next five years.
Right now I'm studying at Clear Mountain Adult
School. These are my plans. First, I'm going to
study nursing at a community college. Next, I'm
going to get a job as a home health aide. Then,
Jean and I are going to get married. Finally, I'm
going to get my nursing degree and become a
registered nurse. I want to have children and work
  part-time as a nurse.

left margin

right margin

E **Read the paragraph again. Look at the underlined words. What do they show?**

F **Write your plans for the next five years.**

First, I plan to _____

Next, _____

Then, _____

Finally, _____

G **Now write a paragraph about your goals on a separate sheet of paper. Follow the example in exercise D.**

LESSON 6 How to find help

GOAL ▶ **Ask for and find help**   *Life Skill*

Where is Ahmed?
Why isn't he sitting
    with the other
    students?
How does he feel?

 Read Ahmed's story.

I need to make plans, but sometimes I have problems. My first day at Clear Mountain Adult School was difficult. I didn't speak English and many students spoke only Spanish or another language. I wanted to go home, but I didn't. I went to school every day. I worked hard and listened carefully. Now I can speak and understand a little.

 Look at some of Ahmed's problems and find the solutions. Draw a line from the problem to the solution. There can be more than one answer.

didn't speak English

didn't have a job

wanted a high school diploma

wanted to go to the library

• asked a friend for help
• looked in the newspaper
• went to school every day
• worked hard and listened carefully
• called for the address
• looked on a map
• talked to a counselor

C Read about Ahmed's problems. In a group, complete the chart with ways for Ahmed to find help.

Problem	Ask a friend	Talk to the police	Go to school	Look in the phone book	Go to the library	Talk to a counselor	Ask the teacher at school	Look in a newspaper
He didn't speak English.	x		x		x			
He didn't have a job.								
He didn't know what to do in an emergency.								
He didn't know where to find information about citizenship.								
He didn't know how to read a bus schedule.								
He needed to find a home for his family.								
He needed to find a school for his children.								

D Share your answers to exercise C with the class.

E What problems did you have when you first came to this country? What did you do?

Problem	Ask a friend	Talk to the police	Go to school	Look in the phone book	Go to the library	Talk to a counselor	Ask the teacher at school	Read a newspaper
Didn't know how to find a doctor.	x			x			x	

GOAL ▶ **Learn about places to learn**   *Life Skill*

A **How can each of these help us to learn? Draw a line from the place to the kind of learning you can do there. There can be more than one answer.**

public library   Get advice on health or legal problems.

Internet   Borrow books or videos.

hotline   Take classes in English, computers, or art.

adult education center   Read the latest news and find jobs.

B **Read the flyer.**

Come to Mountain View Public Library

The Mountain View Public Library has books, videos, and CDs for adults and children of every age. Our staff will help you search our computer catalogs or access the Internet. Our collection includes books in more than forty languages.

Join one of our book discussion groups or try our creative writing workshop. Come to one of our lunchtime lectures to learn how to start your own business or to learn about countries around the world with one of our guest speakers.

For more information about our services, come to the information desk at the main entrance. Our services are free to all state residents.

OPENING HOURS: *Monday–Thursday 9–9, Friday and Saturday 9–5, Sunday 1–5*

C **Make a list of what you can find in the Mountain View Public Library.**

1. *You can borrow books, videos, and CDs.* _____

2. _____

3. _____

4. _____

D **In order to get a library card you must provide identification. Put a check next to each item that you have.**

_____ driver's license   _____ ID card   _____ utility bill

_____ rental receipt   _____ pre-printed checks   _____ passport

E **Fill out the library card application.**

Mountain View Public Library

APPLICATION FOR LIBRARY CARD

Applicant's Name: (please print)

Last _____ First _____ MI __

Applicant's Address:

Number and street _____

City _____ State _____ Zip _____

Home phone: _____ Work phone: _____

E-mail address: _____

Signature _____

Date _____

F **Active Task:** What can you find in your public library? Go to the library or look at their web site.

_____ books   _____ Internet

_____ computers   _____ videos

_____ CDs   _____ courses

G **Active Task:** Go to the library and apply for a library card. Bring your card to class. Tell about your experience.

A Fill in the missing information about the educational system in the United States with words from the box.

| Bachelor's | Associate's | elementary | diploma | community |

Children in the United States start _____ school at six years old. Next, they usually go to a junior high school or middle school and then to a high school. When they finish high school, they receive a _____. After that, they can get a job or go to junior college or a _____ college for two years, where they can get an _____ degree. They can also go to a university for four years and get a _____ degree.

B Match the words with the definitions. Write the correct letter next to each word on the left.

_____ resident   a. finish school or college

_____ vocational   b. person who advises other people

_____ counselor   c. related to studying

_____ academic   d. person who lives in a country or state

_____ graduate   e. related to your job

C Ask three friends about their goals. Write sentences about them.

EXAMPLE:
Mario wants to study auto mechanics so he can start an auto repair business.

1. _____

2. _____

3. _____

Review

D Read about Teresa. Use the words from the box to label the parts of the paragraph.

indent

left margin

title

right margin

My Family

My name is Teresa. I came to the United States two years ago. I don't want to get a job right now. My husband works very hard. He is an auto mechanic here in Chicago. He plans to start his own business soon. We have one daughter. Her name is Graciela. I am going to learn English so I can help her in school. I'm going to help the teacher in Graciela's school. My husband wants to work hard and help our family too. We are going to be good parents.

E Write a similar paragraph about yourself. Remember to use *plan to, want to, going to* in your writing. Choose one of these titles:

1. My Family

2. My Job

3. My Goals

Making a timeline

1. Make groups of three or four.

2. Draw a timeline for your group for the next five years.

3. Each person writes three goals on pieces of paper and puts them on the timeline.

4. Show your timeline to the other groups.

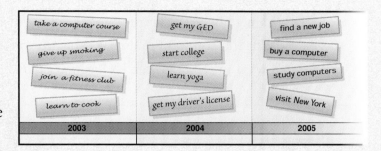

take a computer course	get my GED	find a new job
give up smoking	start college	buy a computer
join a fitness club	learn yoga	study computers
learn to cook	get my driver's license	visit New York
2003	**2004**	**2005**

Portfolio

1. Make a timeline on a large piece of paper. On your timeline, write what you want to do for the next five years. (See pages 145 and 147.)

2. Write a paragraph about your family. (See Unit 1 and page 158.)

3. Write a paragraph about what you are doing now in your life. (See page 92 and page 158.)

4. Write a paragraph about your plans for the next five years. (See page 152.)

5. Show your paragraphs to a friend and ask for comments. Use the comments to improve your writing.

6. Make a cover sheet for your timeline and your paragraphs.

7. Present your portfolio to the class and read your paragraphs.

My
Portfolio
Mario
Hernandez

PRONUNCIATION

Listen to these questions and answers. The words *going to* and *want to* are often joined together in spoken English (but not in writing!). Listen to these examples.

What are you going to do? → What are you *gonna* do?

I am going to study computers. → I'm *gonna* study computers.

What do you want to do? → What do you *wanna* do?

I want to get a new car. → I *wanna* get a new car.

LEARNER LOG

Circle what you learned and write the page number where you learned it.

1. I understand the educational system in the U.S.
   Yes   Maybe   No   Page _____

2. I can talk about my goals.
   Yes   Maybe   No   Page _____

3. I can write a paragraph about my goals.
   Yes   Maybe   No   Page _____

4. I know where to find help and information.
   Yes   Maybe   No   Page _____

5. I can fill out a library application form.
   Yes   Maybe   No   Page _____

6. I can use *want to, plan to,* and *need to.*
   Yes   Maybe   No   Page _____

7. I can use *going to* for the future.
   Yes   Maybe   No   Page _____

Did you answer *No?* Review the information with a partner.

Rank what you like to do best from 1 to 6. 1 is your favorite activity. Your teacher will help you.

☐ practice listening

☐ practice speaking

☐ practice reading

☐ practice writing

☐ learn grammar

☐ learn new words (vocabulary)

I think I improved most in

_____.

Useful Words

Cardinal numbers

1	one
2	two
3	three
4	four
5	five
6	six
7	seven
8	eight
9	nine
10	ten
11	eleven
12	twelve
13	thirteen
14	fourteen
15	fifteen
16	sixteen
17	seventeen
18	eighteen
19	nineteen
20	twenty
21	twenty-one
30	thirty
40	forty
50	fifty
60	sixty
70	seventy
80	eighty
90	ninety
100	one hundred
1000	one thousand
10,000	ten thousand
100,000	one hundred thousand
1,000,000	one million

Ordinal numbers

first	1st
second	2nd
third	3rd
fourth	4th
fifth	5th
sixth	6th
seventh	7th
eighth	8th
ninth	9th
tenth	10th
eleventh	11th
twelfth	12th
thirteenth	13th
fourteenth	14th
fifteenth	15th
sixteenth	16th
seventeenth	17th
eighteenth	18th
nineteenth	19th
twentieth	20th
twenty-first	21st

Days of the week

Sunday
Monday
Tuesday
Wednesday
Thursday
Friday
Saturday

Seasons

winter
spring
summer
fall

Months of the year

January
February
March
April
May
June
July
August
September
October
November
December

Write the date

April 5, 2004 = 4/ 5/ 04

Temperature chart

Degrees Celsius (°C) and
Degrees Fahrenheit (°F)

100°C	212°F
30°C	86°F
25°C	77°F
20°C	68°F
15°C	59°F
10°C	50°F
5°C	41°F
0°C	32°F
−5°C	23°F

Weights and measures

Weight:
1 pound (lb.) = 453.6 grams (g)
16 ounces (oz.) = 1 pound (lb.)
1 pound (lb.) = .45 kilogram (kg)

Liquid or Volume:
1 cup (c.) = .24 liter (l)
2 cups (c.) = 1 pint (pt.)
2 pints = 1 quart (qt.)
4 quarts = 1 gallon (gal.)
1 gallon (gal.) = 3.78 liters (l)

Length:
1 inch (in. or ″) = 2.54 centimeters (cm)
1 foot (ft. or ′) = .3048 meters (m)
12 inches (12″) = 1 foot (1′)
1 yard (yd.) = 3 feet (3′) or 0.9144 meters (m)
1 mile (mi.) = 1609.34 meters (m) or 1.609 kilometers (km)

Time:
60 seconds = 1 minute
60 minutes = 1 hour
24 hours = 1 day
28–31 days = 1 month
12 months = 1 year

The Simple Present – *have*

I, you, we, they	have	three brothers. a cat.
he, she, it	has	free time. black hair.

The Simple Present – *have* (negative)

I, you, we, they	do (don't)	have	children. a dog.
he , she, it	does (doesn't)		free time. blond hair.

The Simple Present – *be*

I	am	Gilberto.
you, we, they	are	a cook.
he, she, it	is	happy. from Brazil.

The Simple Present – *be* (negative)

I	am ('m) not	hungry.
you, we, they	are ('re) not (aren't)	from Mexico.
he, she, it	is ('s) not (isn't)	a student.

The Simple Present – Regular verbs

I, you, we, they	wear buy want	shoes.
he, she, it	wears buys wants	

The Simple Present – Regular verbs (negative)

I, you, we, they	do not (don't)	wear buy want	sandals.
he, she, it	does not (doesn't)		

The Present Continuous

Subject	*be*	+ Verb + *ing*	
I	am	walking	right now.
you, we, they	are	sitting	at this moment.
he, she, it	is	writing	today.

The Simple Past – Regular verbs

Subject	Base + *ed*	Sentence
I, you, we, they, he, she, it	talked	I talked to the doctor.
	walked	She walked to work.
	played	They played football.

The Simple Past – Regular verbs (negative)

Subject	*did + not*	Base	Sentence
I, you, we, they, he, she, it	did not (didn't)	talk	I did not talk with customers.
		answer	She did not answer the phone.
		work	We didn't work in the evenings.

The Simple Past – *be*

Subject	Past	Sentence
I, he, she, it	was	She was a cashier.
you, we, they	were	You were at a hotel.

The Simple Past – *be* (negative)

Subject	Past + *not*	Sentence
I, he, she, it	was not (wasn't)	Dalva wasn't a desk clerk.
you, we, they	were not (weren't)	They weren't at the restaurant.

Grammar Reference

The Modal Verb – *should*

Subject	Modal verb	Base	Sentence
I, you, we, they he, she, it	should	exercise	You should exercise every day.
		eat	They should eat three meals a day.
		sleep	He should sleep eight hours a day.

The Modal Verb – *should* (negative)

Subject	Modal verb	*not*	Base	Sentence
I, you, we, they, he, she, it	should	not (shouldn't)	take	You shouldn't take aspirin.
			drive	They shouldn't drive.
			eat	She shouldn't eat fatty foods.

The Modal Verb – *should* (question form)

Should	Subject	Base	Sentence
should	I, you, we, they he, she, it,	take	Should I take two tablets?
		call	Should we call a doctor?
		go	Should he go to the hospital?

The Modal verb – *can*

Subject	*can*	Base	Sentence
I, you, we, they he, she, it	can	fix	I can fix a car.
		use	They can use a fax machine.
		type	He can type.

The Modal Verb – *can* (negative)

Subject	*cannot = can't*	Base	Sentence
I, you, we, they he, she, it	cannot* (can't)	cook	I can't cook.
		drive	They can't drive.
		speak	She can't speak Spanish.

*Cannot is one word.

The Modal Verb – *can* (question form)

can	Subject	Base	Sentence
can	I, you, we, they, he, she, it	ask	Can I ask a question?
		speak	Can they speak Spanish?
		use	Can he use a computer?

Verb + Infinitive

Subject	Verb	Infinitive (*to* + base)		Sentence
I, you, we, they	want, need, plan	to	graduate	I want to graduate in spring.
			study	We need to study computers.
he, she, it	wants, needs, plans		get	He plans to get a job.

Future – *going to*

Subject	*be + going to*	Base	Sentence
I	am going to	be	I am going to be a nurse.
you, we, they	are going to	work	You are going to work hard.
he, she, it	is going to	save	She is going to save money.

Stand Out 2 Vocabulary List

Pre-Unit
Feelings
Angry (P2)
Happy (P2)
Hungry (P2)
Nervous (P2)
Sad (P2)
Tired (P2)

Unit 1
Weather
Cloudy (3)
Foggy (3)
Rainy (3)
Snowy (3)
Sunny (3)
Windy (3)
Seasons
Fall (5)
Spring (5)
Summer (5)
Winter (5)
Family
Aunt (6)
Brother (6)
Child(ren) (6)
Daughter (9)
Father (6)
Granddaughter (9)
Grandfather (9)
Grandmother (9)
Grandparents (6)
Husband (9)
Mother (6)
Nephew (9)
Niece (9)
Parents (6)
Sister (6)
Son (9)
Uncle (6)
Wife (9)
Colors
Black (11)
Blue (11)
Brown (11)
Gray (11)
Green (11)
Orange (30)
Pink (30)
Red (11)
Yellow (30)

Unit 2
Clothing
Baseball cap (24)

Blouse (22)
Boots (24)
Coat (21)
Dress (22)
Glove (24)
Jacket (21)
Jeans (21)
Pajamas (21)
Pants (21)
Raincoat (22)
Sandals (21)
Scarf (24)
Shirt (21)
Shoe (22)
Shorts (24)
Skirt (22)
Sneaker (22)
Sock (21)
Suit (27)
Sunglasses (24)
Sweater (21)
Swimsuit (28)
Tie (21)
T-shirt (24)

Unit 3
Food
Apples (41)
Beef (42)
Bread (46)
Butter (41)
Cake mix (46)
Carrots (41)
Cheese (41)
Chicken (41)
Fish (41)
Flour (46)
Ground beef (48)
Hamburger (49)
Ice cream (48)
Jam (48)
Lettuce (41)
Milk (46)
Oil (48)
Orange (48)
Salad (43)
Sandwich (43)
Soup (48)
Spaghetti (41)
Tomato (46)
Containers and units
Bag (48)
Bottle (48)
Box (48)
Can (48)

Carton (48)
Gallon (48)
Jar (48)
Loaf (loaves) (48)
Pound (48)

Unit 4
Housing and rooms
Apartment (61)
Balcony (68)
Bedroom (66)
Bathroom (66)
Condominium (62)
Dining room (66)
Kitchen (66)
House (61)
Living room (66)
Mobile home (62)
Pool (68)
Yard (66)
Furniture
Armchair (73)
Bed (73)
Bookcase (73)
Chair (73)
Coffee table (73)
Counter (75)
Dining room set (73)
Dishwasher (72)
Dresser (73)
Lamp (73)
Microwave (72)
Oven (72)
Refrigerator (69)
Sink (75)
Sofa (73)
Stove (72)
Table (75)
Trash can (78)
TV (76)
Wardrobe (73)
Washer/dryer (72)
VCR (76)

Unit 5
Buildings
Bank (63)
Bowling alley (81)
Courthouse (83)
Department store (83)
Factory (81)
Fire station (83)
Gas station (83)
Hardware store (83)
Hospital (83)

Library (83)
Mall (81)
Movie theater (81)
Museum (89)
Pharmacy (83)
Police station (83)
Post office (83)
Restaurant (83)
Supermarket (46)

Unit 6
Parts of the body
Arm (103)
Back (103)
Chest (103)
Ear (104)
Eye (103)
Foot (feet) (103)
Hand (103)
Head (103)
Heart (103)
Leg (103)
Mouth (103)
Neck (103)
Nose (103)
Shoulder (103)
Stomach (103)
Throat (104)
Tongue (104)

Tooth (teeth) (104)
Illnesses
Backache (105)
Headache (105)
Sore throat (105)
Stomachache (105)
Toothache (105)
Medicines
Antacid (111)
Aspirin (111)
Cough syrup (111)

Unit 7
Jobs
Administrative assistant (128)
Cashier (123)
Cook (44)
Custodian (123)
Delivery person (123)
Dentist (90)
Doctor (123)
Driver (126)
Gardener (123)
Homemaker (123)
Manager (126)
Mechanic (123)
Police officer (123)
Salesperson (27)
Student (122)

Office machines
Answering machine (135)
Computer (135)
Copier (135)
Fax (135)
Printer (135)
Shredder (135)

Unit 8
Education
Adult school (143)
Associate's degree (144)
Bachelor's degree (144)
Career (142)
Community college (144)
Diploma (144)
Elementary school (143)
GED (general equivalency diploma) (144)
Goal (141)
Graduate (145)
Junior college (144)
Junior high school (143)
High school (143)
Middle school (143)
Trade school (143)
University (141)

Stand Out 2 Irregular Verb List
The following verbs are used in *Stand Out 2* and have irregular forms in the simple past.

Base Form	Simple Past	Base Form	Simple Past
be	was, were	have	had
break	broke	make	made
buy	bought	put	put
can	could	read	read
come	came	run	ran
cut	cut	say	said
do	did	sleep	slept
draw	drew	speak	spoke
drink	drank	swim	swam
eat	ate	take	took
find	found	wake	woke
get	got	wear	wore
go	went	write	wrote

Stand Out 2 Listening Scripts

Pre-Unit

p. P3, Lesson 3, exercise B
1. c   2. G   3. b   4. F   5. y

p. P3, Lesson 3, exercise C
1. My first name is Esteban. E-S-T-E-B-A-N
2. My last name is Garcia. G-A-R-C-I-A
3. I live on Tremont Street. T-R-E-M-O-N-T
4. I live in Sausalito. S-A-U-S-A-L-I-T-O
5. I am from Mexico. M-E-X-I-C-O
6. My teacher's last name is Parelli. P-A-R-E-L-L-I

p. P4, Lesson 4, exercise B
1. 7   2. 14   3. 0   4. 30
5. 22   6. 100   7. 16   8. 5

p. P4, Lesson 4, exercise C
1. 619–555–6391   2. 312–555–5100
3. 786–555–2852   4. 915–555–5280
5. 323–555–3967   6. 347–555–1743

p. P5, Lesson 5, exercise B
Point to your book.
Stand up.
Talk to your partner.
Sit down.
Write your name.
Read your partner's name.

Unit 1

p. 4, Lesson 2, exercise E
(Voice of a radio announcer) Hello, everyone! Today's international weather map shows that Mexico City is cloudy with temperatures around 77 (degrees). A beautiful day in the city of Port-au-Prince! Port-au-Prince is sunny with warm temperatures at 85 (degrees). To the south, Rio de Janeiro is a sunny 95 (degrees). We find that Ho Chi Minh City is cloudy with a temperature of 90 (degrees) and the weather in Tokyo is rainy with a daytime temperature of 46 (degrees). Wear a warm hat if you're in Moscow! Moscow is cloudy and very cold with a temperature of 15 (degrees). Today's national weather report shows that New York City is snowy with a temperature of 32 (degrees). Chicago is also snowy today with a cold temperature of 21 (degrees). Los Angeles is foggy today with temperatures around 64 (degrees) and San Francisco is windy with daytime temperatures at around 54 (degrees). That's all for now. We'll be back with international weather updates in one hour!

Unit 2

p. 30, Lesson 5, exercise C
1. This brother is wearing green pants.
2. This brother is wearing black shoes.
3. This brother is wearing a plaid shirt and sandals.
4. This brother is wearing blue jeans.
5. This brother is wearing red sneakers.
6. This brother is wearing a striped shirt.

p. 32 , Lesson 6, exercise B
Radio Announcer: Come to Sam's Uniform Clothing Store Tuesday, Wednesday, and Thursday! We're having an end of the season blowout sale! D'you want to save money? Of course you do! Listen carefully for special coupon savings on select clothing.

1. Come to Sam's Uniform Clothing Store for great price savings on men's shirts! Men's shirts are now $22 with a coupon from this week's newspaper. You save $3! Great deal!
2. Today and tomorrow only, all Sam's sneakers on sale for only $15.40. No coupon necessary! Bring the whole family!
3. Big savings this month at Sam's Uniform Clothing Store! Women's pants, regularly $45, are on sale for only $36! Come in now before this offer ends.
4. We have baseball caps for every fan at Sam's. Special savings for every purchase made with a Sam's coupon. Look for coupons in the mail or in your local newspaper. One coupon for each baseball cap in this special offer.

p. 40, Pronunciation
1. 40 dollars   2. 17 dollars   3. 80 dollars

Unit 3

p. 43, Lesson 2, exercise B
1. Server: Good afternoon, sir. Ready to order?
   Customer: Yes, thanks. I'm very hungry.
   Server: We'll take care of that. What would you like?
   Customer: Well, I would like the Super Burger.
   Server: Great, the Super Burger "Combo"—right?
   Customer: Yes. Can I have a dinner salad too?
   Server: Sure. Your food will be coming right up.
   Customer: Thanks.

2. Server: Hello. Can I take your order?
   Customer: Yes. We would like two sirloin steaks—rare with potatoes and the vegetable of the day.
   Server: OK, two sirloin steak lunches. Do you want a dinner salad with that?
   Customer: No, thank you, but please hurry. We have an appointment in an hour.
   Server: What would you like to drink?
   Customer: Water is fine thanks.

3. Server: Hi, are you about ready?
   Customer: Yes, can I have the Caesar salad, please?
   Server: Sure. Anything to drink?
   Customer: Yes, a glass of milk would be great.
   Server: OK, the Caesar and a milk.
   Customer: Oh, and how about some fruit on the side?
   Server: Sounds good. It will be only a few minutes.
   Customer: Thanks.

p. 55, Lesson 7, exercise B
On Thursdays Augustin and Silvia are not busy at the restaurant. They make a shopping list every Thursday

morning. Today they don't have to buy a lot of food at the store. Augustin says they need ground beef. Silvia says they don't need turkey, and they don't need tuna fish or chicken. Augustin says they need ham and bacon. Silvia says they don't need lettuce, carrots, or tomatoes and they don't need fresh fruit, sugar, or flour.

Augustin doesn't like to shop for food, but he wants to help Silvia. Silvia doesn't shop for food because she works many hours at the restaurant. Silvia and Augustin try to help each other. Augustin doesn't like to shop but he shops anyway, so his wife is happy. They are not a rich couple, but they are a happy couple.

Unit 4

p. 63, Lesson 2, exercise B
Bank Clerk: May I help you, sir?
Kyung: I would like to open an account. What do I need to do?
Bank Clerk: Well, first, I need to know your name and address.
Kyung: My name is Kyung Kim, and I live at 33457 Akron Street, Arcadia, Florida 34265.
Bank Clerk: Thank you, sir. Your information is going in the computer now. Next, what kind of account do you want?
Kyung: I will need both a savings and a checking account. I want to save money, but I'll need a checking account to pay my bills, isn't that right?
Bank Clerk: Yes, that's correct. I will need two forms of ID.
Kyung: Two forms?
Bank Clerk: Yes, two. One picture ID and one other ID. Your picture ID can be a passport, driver's license, or a residence card. The other ID can be a utility bill or an official ID with your name. You'll need to make deposit, too.
Kyung: How about a paycheck from work?
Bank Clerk: That's fine. Your account is now open and the checks will come to your home in a few days.
Kyung: Thanks. I appreciate your help.

p. 70, Lesson 5, exercise A
Kyung: Excuse me, I need help.
Agent: What can I do for you?
Kyung: I need a three-bedroom house immediately.
Agent: How much can you spend?
Kyung: I need to find a house for $900 or less.
Agent: OK. I think we can help you. Do you want to be near schools and stores?
Kyung: Yes, I want to be near schools, but it isn't necessary.
Agent: All right. And do you have pets?
Kyung: No, I don't. But maybe I can get a dog . . .
Agent: I see. Do you WANT a house with a big yard or do you NEED one?
Kyung: I guess I WANT one; I don't have a dog right now.
Agent: Do you want a two-story or a one-story house?
Kyung: I want a one story because I don't like stairs.
Agent: I have one house, but it doesn't have a garage.

Kyung: I need a garage. That won't do.
Agent: Well, I'm sorry. That's all we have right now. I will call you when other homes are available.
Kyung: OK. Thank you for your help.

p.75, Lesson 7, exercise A
Lin: Where do you want the table, Mom?
Nam-young: Please put the table in the corner. And be careful—it's heavy!
Sung: And the toaster?
Nam-young: Put the toaster on the kitchen counter, please.
Kyung: Let's see. I have a clock here.
Nam-young: Oh, good. I want to put the clock over the refrigerator.
Sung: That looks like everything for the kitchen.
Nam-young: Thanks, but I need the trash can. Oh! It's under the sink!

Unit 5

p. 91, Lesson 5, exercise C
Ex. Attendant: Hello. Jefferson Street Post Office.
Raquel: Hi. I need to send some letters to my family in Brazil tonight. Can I buy stamps there in the evening?
Attendant: No, this post office closes at 5 P.M., but the post office on East Broadway is open tonight.
Raquel: That's great. What is the address again?
Attendant: It is at 151 East Broadway.
Raquel: OK. Do you know the phone number there?
Attendant: Yes, it's 555–6245.
Raquel: Thanks for your help. Goodbye.

1. Raquel: Hello, I want to get a new library card and borrow some books to read. Can you give me your address and directions to the library?
Librarian: Sure. We are at 125 East Broadway, next to the park.
Raquel: Thanks. And could you tell me your phone number? I got your number from the operator and forgot to write it down.
Librarian: No problem. Happy to help. It's 555–7323.

2. Raquel: Hello. I just arrived here from Brazil. I need help understanding my visa. Who can I talk to?
Operator: Hmm. You need to talk to Immigration and Naturalization right here in City Hall. I will transfer you. Please hold.
Immigration Assistant: Immigration and Naturalization Agency. How can I be of assistance?
Raquel: Yes. I'd like to make an appointment to discuss my visa.
Immigration Assistant: How's next Monday at 9 A.M.?
Raquel: Excellent. Thanks. Could you tell me where you're located?
Immigration Assistant: We're at City Hall on 160 West Broadway. Our phone number is 555–3305.

3. Raquel: I need to find out about getting a driver's license. Can you give me some information?
DMV: Yes, of course. You have to make an appointment. I'll give you the number. Do you have a pen?

Raquel: Yes, go ahead.
DMV: The number is 555–2778.
Raquel: OK! Great! Where is the office located?
DMV: It's 375 Western Avenue. Opening hours are 8:30 A.M. to 4:00 P.M.
Raquel: OK, great, thanks.

4. Police Desk: Police department.
Raquel: Hi. I lost my purse on the bus yesterday. Do you think someone turned it in?
Police desk: Hold on, I'll transfer your call to the lost and found.
Raquel: Thank you.
Desk: Lost and found.
Raquel: Hi. I lost my purse on the bus yesterday. Do you think someone turned it in?
Desk: You'll have to come in to our office to identify it.
Raquel: OK, what's your address?
Desk: It's 140 Broadway.
Raquel: And what's your number?
Desk: 555–4869.
Raquel: Thank you. Goodbye.

Unit 6
p. 104, Lesson 2, exercise D
Conversation 1
Patient: I'm a little worried.
Dr.: Why? You seem to be doing fine.
Patient: I don't see well at night.
Dr.: When people get older, sometimes they have trouble seeing.
Patient: Is there anything I can do?
Dr.: Yes, of course. I will check your eyes and prescribe glasses if it's necessary.

Conversation 2
Patient: Good morning, Doctor.
Dr.: Good morning, Alexi. Are you in a lot of pain?
Patient: Yes, doctor. I sure am. All I can eat is soup.
Dr.: You have some bad cavities. Your teeth look very bad.
Patient: I don't understand it. I brush every day.
Dr.: Sometimes there are problems, and brushing isn't enough.
Patient: I never had problems with my teeth before.
Dr.: Don't worry. We'll take care of everything.

Conversation 3
Dr.: Say "ahhh." (*Alexi says "ahh"*) Yep, you have a red throat.
Patient: Yeah, I thought I was sick. I have a terrible sore throat.
Dr.: You will be OK. Just take some cough syrup before you go to bed every night.
Patient: How long will this last?
Dr.: You should be OK in a week.
Patient: Doctor, can I go to work?
Dr.: Go ahead, but don't talk a lot. Talking will irritate your throat more.

Conversation 4
Patient: Doctor, this cold is terrible. My nose is running and I'm so tired.
Dr.: You may have the flu. Let's take your temperature.
Patient: Do you think I have a fever?
Dr.: We will soon find out.
Patient: Should I stay home from work?
Dr.: If you have the flu, that might be a good idea. You will need to get plenty of rest and drink lots of fluids.
Patient: Whatever you say, Doctor.

p. 106, exercise B
Receptionist: Good afternoon. Alliance Medical Offices. How can I help you?
Alexi: I need to make an appointment with Dr. Singh.
Recep.: Very good. What's your name?
Alexi: Alexi Tashkov.
Recep: And Alexi, are you a new patient?
Alexi: Yes.
Recep: Why do you want to see the doctor?
Alexi: I'm tired all the time.
Recep: What's your date of birth?
Alexi: June 28, 1961.
Recep: Where do you live?
Alexi: 1427 Hamilton Street, New York City, zip code 12101.
Recep: What's your phone number?
Alexi: 212–555–5755.
Recep: When can you see the doctor?
Alexi: Anytime on Monday or Tuesday.
Recep: Dr. Singh will see you at 10 A.M. on Tuesday.
Alexi: Fine. Thank you.
Recep: How will you pay? Do you have insurance?
Alexi: No, I don't. I'll pay by check.
Recep: That's fine, thank you.
Alexi: Goodbye.

p. 107, Lesson 3, exercise C
Conversation 1
Medical Receptionist: Hello. Can I help you?
Patient: Yes this is Ming Nguyen. M-I-N-G N-G-Y-Y-E-N. I need an appointment. I have terrible headaches every day.
Med. Recep: Every day?
Patient: Yes, every day for a week.
Med. Recep: Can you come in at 3:00 P.M. today?
Patient: That would be fine.
Med. Recep: Do you have insurance?
Patient: No, I will pay cash.
Med. Recep: Sounds good. We will see you at 3:00.
Patient: Thanks. Good-bye.

Conversation 2
Med. Receptionist: Hello, Dr. Angelo's office. What can I do for you?
Patient: I need an appointment as soon as possible.
Med. Recep: Is this an emergency?
Patient: No, not really. I need to see him about the stomachaches that I have after I eat certain foods.
Med. Recep: OK. You can come in next Monday at 2:00 in the afternoon.

Patient: Sounds fine, but isn't there anything any earlier?
Med. Recep: I'm afraid not. What's your name?
Patient: My name is Michael Chan, C-H-A-N. Do you take credit cards?
Med. Recep: Yes, we do. We take all major credit cards.
Patient: Thanks. I'll see you then. Good-bye.

Conversation 3
Med. Recep: Hello, can you hold?
Patient: No, this is very important. My brother Antonio Marco is a regular patient with you and he is having a very bad toothache. He also has a fever.
Med. Recep: Come right in.
Patient: Right now?
Med. Recep: Yes, right now.
Patient: Thanks! We have dental insurance.
Med. Recep: Excellent. We will be waiting for you.

Conversation 4
Med. Recep: Hello, Dr. Albert's office. Can I help you?
Patient: Yes. My throat hurts a lot.
Med. Recep: Do you want an appointment?
Patient: Yes, I do.
Med. Recep: Are you a new patient?
Patient: No. My name is Sam Hosker. H-O-S-K-E-R. I was there last week for a physical.
Med. Recep: Oh, yes, Mr. Hosker. When can you come in?
Patient: I can come in at 6:00 today.
Med. Recep: That's a little late, but I think the doctor can see you then.
Patient: Can I pay by check?
Med. Recep: Yes, of course.
Patient: Thanks very much.

p. 108, Lesson 4, exercise A
My name is Alexi Tashkov. I thought I was very healthy because I did many things to take care of my health. For example, I walked a mile every day. I talked to a doctor every year and I played soccer on the weekends. I had a lot of energy for a while, but I had one very bad habit. I smoked a pack of cigarettes every day!

p. 108, Lesson 4, exercise B
After three years, my life changed. I was tired a lot in 1999. I went to the doctor, and he said to stop smoking. I didn't know smoking was bad for my heart. He said it was very dangerous to smoke because I could get cancer or a heart attack. I continued to smoke and three months later I had a heart attack.

p. 115, Lesson 7, exercise B
Now, Gilberto, I want you to listen closely. I know you don't want high blood pressure. There are a few things you need to do. I know you did these things before. Now you have to be very careful. You need to exercise every day. Don't do too much. Maybe 30 minutes. One thing you can do is walk. You should walk every day and run every two days. You will be tired for a while, but don't sleep too much. You should get eight hours of sleep every night. Try not to sleep more than eight hours. Eat good foods. No fatty foods. You should take your medicine every day and of course DON'T SMOKE ever again.

Unit 7
p. 127, Lesson 3, exercise C
Esteban: Gloria, I really need a job and right away. I don't speak a lot of English and don't have much experience but I really know I can work hard. What do you think I should do?
Gloria: Let's look in the newspaper and see what we can find.
E: Good idea. I have the "Daily News" right here.
G: Good, let's find the classified ads and then find the employment section.
E: Here it is.
(1) E: Here's one. It says "no experience" and it pays $6 an hour. Maybe I should call them.
(2) G: That sounds great, but you should look at full-time jobs, too. For example, do you type? You could work in an office.
(3) E: No, I don't type. Here's one that says they will train me to cook. I love to eat so maybe this is the best job for me. Only they don't say anything about the pay.
(4) G: Maybe you should be a driver. You can do that job with no problem. You have a driver's license and can follow directions. You work hard, too.
E: That's the job for me. I'm going to apply for the driver position.

Unit 8
p. 141, Lesson 1, exercise A
My name is Lien Bui. I am from Vietnam. I came to the United States two years ago. I have many plans for my education and I want to do many things in the future. My goal is to be a counselor for adults. Maybe I can work in an adult school or a college in the future. Right now I want to speak English better. Also, I want a better job. Right now, I work at night and I am very tired all the time, so I don't like my job. I plan to get my high school diploma, and then I want to go to college to study counseling. I need to attend university to be a counselor. When I graduate, I want to get a good job. I want to keep that job and maybe buy a house or condo with the money because I don't like my neighborhood now. The streets are dirty and dangerous. I want to move to a safer place when I get a new job and enough money. I don't know if I'm going to get married or become a U.S. citizen, but I know I need a good education.

Stand Out 2 Skills Index